NARCISSISM AND NARCISSISTIC ABUSE RECOVERY

Free Yourself by Understanding the Narcissists Personality Disorder, What the Hell Happened in Your Relationship and How to Effectively Heal

Diana Ortega

© **Copyright 2019 - All rights reserved.**

The content contained within this book may not be reproduced, duplicated, or transmitted without direct written permission from the author or the publisher.

Under no circumstances will any blame or legal responsibility be held against the publisher, or author, for any damages, reparation, or monetary loss due to the information contained within this book. Either directly or indirectly.

Legal Notice:

This book is copyright protected. This book is only for personal use. You cannot amend, distribute, sell, use, quote or paraphrase any part, or the content within this book, without the consent of the author or publisher.

Disclaimer Notice:

Please note the information contained within this document is for educational and entertainment purposes only. All effort has been executed to present accurate, up to date, and reliable, complete information. No warranties of any kind are declared or implied. Readers acknowledge that the author is not engaging in the rendering of legal, financial, medical or professional advice. The content within this book has been derived from various sources. Please consult a licensed professional before attempting any techniques outlined in this book.

By reading this document, the reader agrees that under no circumstances is the author responsible for any losses, direct or indirect, which are incurred as a result of the use of information contained within this document, including, but not limited to, — errors, omissions, or inaccuracies.

Table of Contents

Introduction 6
What is a Narcissist? 8
A Relationship with a Narcissist 15
The Birth of a Narcissist 21
How Narcissists Choose Their Victims 29
The Cycle of Narcissistic Abuse 42
   Fundamentals of Narcissistic Abuse & Cognitive Dissonance 48
The Narcissists Arsenal 53
   Love bombing 53
   Manipulation 54
   Projection 55
   Language 56
   Cognitive dissonance 58
Narcissist's Language 63
Hardships of Escaping an Abusive Relationship 69
Breaking Free From a Narcissistic Partner: Strategies and Advice 75
Detachment 84
The Healing Process 92
Conclusion 104

Introduction

Love is a beautiful feeling that changes not only our demeanor but also how we see the world. Many times, relationships lift and transform us into better versions of ourselves. Unfortunately, relationships can also bring us down, if we end up putting our trust into the wrong type of people, those that live their whole life caring for one single thing: themselves. We call these people narcissists, and we'll learn later on how we can differentiate them from regular selfish people and what makes them so dangerous, not just as life partners but as "humans" in general.

Are we to blame for entrusting a narcissist with our hearts? No. Anyone, no matter how strong or smart, can fall into the trap of a narcissist. They are first-class manipulators that know how to get under your skin and make themselves detrimental to your survival. They know the game and how to play it, and they never stop playing it.

A relationship with a narcissist never works out well. No matter how hard you try to please or change them, you'll always be the "bad guy" and he or she the victim. Whatever you do will never be good enough, until your confidence melts away and you become a shadow of the person you once were. A relationship with a narcissist is one that you have to escape from and never look back on.

On a positive note, you are not alone. There have been people before you, that have fought and won. That managed to gain control of their lives and regain their happiness. People that are doing it now, alongside you, cutting ties with the most toxic people and starting their journey of healing. There will be people doing it in the future because as long as there are narcissists in our world, there will be victims.

No matter who you are, you can break free, and you can heal. It takes time, effort, a strong will, and hard work, but the pain will slowly diminish in intensity. Until all that's left of it is a life-changing experience, a new you and an awareness of 'red flag' people.

This book aims to help you understand what type of person you unknowingly let in your life, how they become like that, why you didn't see it from the very start, how they weaseled their way into your mind and caused damage that you might not even be aware of… But, most importantly, it aims to be a guide to rebuilding your life from the ground up and recovering from your traumatizing experience.

What is a Narcissist?

We all have people in our lives that are incredibly confident and think highly of themselves. But, while they might not be the most pleasant sort to have around, these people are at best egocentric, if they do manage to have a relatively normal life. Narcissists, on the other hand, have many problems in multiple areas of their life, such as work, relationships, and finances. So, what's the difference between a self-centered person and a narcissist? Why can one have a normal life while the other struggles?

First things first, narcissism is a personality disorder, that one is not born with but develops over time, in certain conditions. A person that has narcissistic personality disorder is described as having a visceral need for attention, an inflated sense of self-importance masking fragile self-esteem, and, perhaps the most notable of all, a complete lack of empathy for others. Empathy is the human trait that allows us to relate to other people's feelings and understand them. Without empathy, one is unable to build authentic human relationships. That is why a narcissist will never have healthy relationships, be it romantic or of other nature.

According to a study published in the *Journal of Clinical Psychiatry,* 7.7% of men, and 4.8% of women develop narcissistic personality disorder (NPD) in their lifetime. The study also determined that young adults, people that went through divorce or separation from their partner, and people of color had higher chances of becoming narcissists (Nordqvist, 2018). We can conclude that technically speaking; if the right conditions are met, anyone can become a narcissist, regardless of sex, race, or age; which comes as a contradiction to the popular belief that only males can be narcissists.

Now let's further focus on the traits of a narcissist, to understand the magnitude of this personality disorder fully, and at the end of this chapter, we'll see how it stands out from other well-known personality disorders such as psychopathy and sociopathy.

An exaggerated sense of self-importance

The self-importance that a narcissist experience is different from vanity or extreme confidence. It's best described as "grandiosity," which defines a sense of superiority built on unrealistic terms. Narcissists believe that they are unique and seek to associate themselves with people/places/situations of high status, as they perceive themselves as being too good for ordinary or average things. This sense of being better than others is often built inside their mind and not based on real-life achievements. They will expect others to treat them as if they are superior, and to do that; they will resort to lying about their abilities, achievements, and always paint themselves as being the better person in any situation, be it relationships or work-related.

In short, a narcissist plays the part of the superior one, in all aspects of life, and will resort to anything to maintain this status, including lying, twisting and diminishing others.

The constant need for attention and validation

While they do foster that sense of superiority, they are somewhat aware of the illusory aspect of it. This is why they need constant praise and recognition to keep the illusion alive. For a narcissist, compliments are not enough. They will seek people that will offer them constant validation, and that will cater to their needs at all times, without ever giving anything back. They expect the people around them to put them on a pedestal, and even the slightest of critiques will be taken as a personal attack and will result in the narcissist becoming abusive.

A relationship with a narcissist can only be one-sided. They are too self-absorbed and cannot put themselves in their partner's shoes and understand their feelings and emotions.

Entitlement

Despite them not being deserving of any special treatment, a narcissist will feel abnormally entitled to the finer things in life. They will expect people to act in a certain way and always be at their disposal. Anyone that does not comply with that will be met with some form of aggression, going as far as being cut from the narcissist's life. They believe that they deserve everything they wish for, and they are not afraid to show it.

Exploiting the people in their life

As we touched on briefly at the start of this chapter, narcissists are incapable of feeling empathy, almost like an empty vessel. For a narcissist, the people in their lives are only a means to an end, more like tools and objects than actual human beings. They do anything to satisfy their own needs, and they will resort to exploiting the people in their life, without feeling any remorse, guilt, or shame for it. This is why it is extremely dangerous to have a narcissist in your life. It is hard to truly understand how someone is incapable of feeling empathy, remorse, or guilt as these are all emotions most people experience, and we automatically assume all humans have.

Narcissists have no problem with exploiting anyone, in any situation, as long as they get what they want, and they will never take responsibility for hurting others. They will keep 'stonewalling' (avoiding answering questions, take responsibility for their actions as if you are speaking to a wall) you until you are confused and docile. All the relationships they build are based on their needs. They will often ensure that they have multiple people to cater to their needs, be it shelter, money, sex, or other sorts of favors.

Living in an imaginary world

A narcissist has a very frail relationship with reality. He or she prefers to live in their own fantasy world in which they can paint whatever image of themselves they want, pushing aside any details that don't work in their favor. They are willingly lying to themselves to protect the feeling of superiority that's detrimental to their survival, and annihilating contradictions or facts that go against their warped logic. Because they are insecure deep inside, this fantasy world works as their means of facing an unsatisfying reality. It allows them to feed their superiority with illusions of success, fame, popularity, and whatever they might need, and their defensive systems react heavily whenever something threatens or tries to reveal the illusion.

Putting others down to lift themselves up

The inner core of the narcissist is threatened by anyone that has something they lack, be it money, success, or simply the admiration of others. They will do anything to diminish a person that threatens their self-importance, by acting condescending, using insults, bullying, and any other means available to 'scoop out' someone's self-worth. No matter how much they end up hurting people, narcissists only care about keeping their own fantasies alive, and will never feel remorseful or take responsibility for their actions.

Monopolizing

A conversation with a narcissist is pretty much like watching TV. They like to be the center of attention, and they will do whatever they can to have the last word, even if that means cutting others short or acting as if others have nothing valuable to say. Everything must revolve around them, no matter what, and they will display strong feelings of envy whenever they are not the focal point of a situation.

With a narcissist, everything is one-sided: relationships, conversations, situations. Simply because they are solely interested in themselves, and anything else only matters if they can use it to their own benefit.

Unstable mood

Whenever they find themselves slipping from their fantasy and face how far from the perfect persona they actually are, a narcissist will display a wide range of emotions. They will feel vulnerable, sad, and might even experience episodes of depression. Also, because of their weak ability to cope with reality, they have a tough time adapting to change or new situations, and they handle stress poorly. In the last effort to protect themselves, narcissists will lash out to the people around them, abusing them to regain that sense of superiority and control that they need. They won't back down from anything if it means that their illusion is kept alive. This fragility combined with their lack of empathy, remorse, and guilt makes the narcissist a toxic, abusive factor in any relationship, no matter how hard the other person may try to please them.

There is a great deal of confusion regarding three well-known types of personality disorders, that being narcissism, psychopathy, and sociopathy. What sets them apart from each other? How do we know what we are dealing with?

Both psychopathy and sociopathy are considered special types of personality disorders called antisocial personality disorders. They share multiple traits such as deceitfulness, aggression, irritability, a tendency towards committing criminal acts, lack of remorse or empathy in general, and not being able to take responsibility for their actions.

What sets them apart from the very beginning is that psychopaths are born while sociopaths are made. What does that mean? It is widely agreed that, although environmental factors, traumas, and different types of abuse influence both disorders, psychopathy is the main result of a faulty development in the parts of the brain that deal with emotions and impulse control. Psychopaths lack emotions and an ability to comprehend emotional responses from early infancy while sociopaths are results of trauma, and they can develop this disorder in any stage of their life. The rates of sociopathy are quite high. Statistically, 1 in 25 US citizens is a sociopath, which is very grim.

Narcissists share some traits with these antisocial disorders such as the lack of empathy and their inflated sense of self, but they are usually not aggressive in a physical way, and they are not impulsive. A narcissist's aggression comes from their verbal abuse and manipulation and is rarely physical. Their need to be admired by others, and thus their dependence on other people's attention also sets them apart from the field of antisocial personality disorders. Out of the two, we could say that narcissism most resembles sociopathy, seeing as it is a disorder that comes as a result of multiple factors and is not caused by undeveloped brain functions. It's only the narcissist's desire to achieve "perfection" that makes him less likely to commit criminal acts, that distinctively sets them apart from the destructive sociopath.

Knowing what a narcissist is, and what it's not, is crucial if you want to understand the sort of person that you have or had next to you, and how to successfully break free from them. Don't forget that, their lack of empathy makes it impossible to have a healthy relationship with them, so it's not your fault that it didn't work out. You deserve to be happy and loved, as much as anyone else in this world, so never feel guilty about leaving a narcissist behind.

A Relationship with a Narcissist

Any sort of relationship with a narcissist brings upon challenges, especially if we are talking about a romantic one. What they look for in a partner is a supply, not an equal. And in their quest of satisfying their own needs, they will end up destroying you, both mentally and emotionally. That's because, at the end of the day, the more broken and vulnerable you are, the more likely you're to remain in that relationship, a prisoner to a cruel and unsympathetic torturer that takes pleasure in your misery.

The best way to describe what effect a relationship with a narcissist will have on you is by using a popular analogy. Have you heard of the frog and the pot of water analogy? If a frog jumps into a pot of boiling water, it will immediately jump out, because it will perceive it as painful and dangerous. The sudden increase in temperature is easily recognizable for the frog. But what if our frog jumps into the water before we put it on the stove? It will feel rather pleasant to stay in room temperature water, right? What if, then we start to gradually heat the water until it reaches its boiling point? What happens to the frog? Unfortunately, it will remain in the water until its untimely death, because it is much harder for the frog to perceive the gradual slight increase in temperature. In other words, you wouldn't jump into a relationship with a person that is obviously selfish, emotionless, and self-centered, but you would stay in a relationship that starts off exciting and romantic but gradually withers away over time. And you would do it out of love. However, just like our frog, a part of you will die along with the relationship, as the boiling waters of narcissism will melt away your confidence, self-worth, and love for yourself.

Another way to look at a narcissistic relationship is to compare it with the old Chinese torture and execution method known as "death by a thousand cuts." In this practice, a knife is used to slowly and methodically cut away portions of someone's body, over a prolonged period of time, until the victim finally succumbs to its fate. It's cruel, atrocious, and unfortunately, the best way to describe narcissistic abuse. A narcissist will slowly cut away pieces of the image you have of yourself, until your whole identity "dies," leaving behind just a doll that the narcissist can move and play with as they please. This is because of their deep insecurities mixed with their desire to control you.

Now let's take it back a notch and understand how a relationship with a narcissist develops, and what are some tell-tale signs that you are in a relationship with a person that has NPD.

You must understand that a narcissist knows how to act in order to make themselves desirable. They are charming and captivating, drawing you in with their boisterous display of personality. They have a cunning capacity for "reading people" and finding out exactly what they want from a romantic partner. Once they have you "figured out," they will perfectly emulate your ideal man/woman until they get you to fall in love with them. These stages of pre-relationship and early relationship are the pinnacle of your love story. These moments will bring you genuine happiness, bliss, and the sense that you have found your soulmate. You will feel like you are in your own romance book/movie, and everything will seem perfect. The narcissist will shower you with compliments, gifts, their undivided attention, and they will cater to your needs. Perhaps this sounds all familiar to you. But, once they are confident that you have fallen in love with them, they will begin to change. Gradually, the water will start heating up, while you bathe in the pot, unaware of the impending danger.

The exciting honeymoon period will abruptly stop as the narcissist starts to display self-centered behaviors. As Dr. W. Keith

Campbell, an expert in NPD, explains, "The effects of narcissism are most substantial in relation to interpersonal functioning. In general, trait narcissism is associated with behaving in such a way that one is perceived as more likable in initial encounters with strangers— but this likability diminishes with time and increased exposure to the narcissistic individual." Once the magical dust clears off, it will already be too late for the partner. At this point, they will start playing their manipulative games, exploiting you and your trust for their own needs. Transforming a love story into a one-sided play in which you will feel lonelier than ever, as the narcissist starts controlling your life and pushing your family and friends away.

The abuse is subtle (ambient abuse) but deadly as they start off by making you feel special and amazing, following by a malicious spur of words and actions meant to devalue you as a person and bring you down. You will always be the one at fault, the inferior one. Your achievements will be diminished or ignored. Your entire existence will seem more of an annoyance to the narcissist, and, once you start denying him or her the recognition or satisfaction they demand, they will discard you. It could be a gradual process, where they start planting the seed of the break-up with remarks and cheating sprees, or it could be abrupt and without reason. Either way, a relationship with a narcissist almost never ends there. They will keep tabs on you and try to get back in your life whenever they are in need of immediate gratification, only to discard you again afterward. This will happen as many times as you allow it to, which is why it is so difficult to escape narcissistic abuse. Especially after they have already brought you to the most vulnerable point in your life, the amount of power and effort to refuse them is enormous. You will *want* to forgive them and give them a second chance. NPD sufferers know how to target their victims, and they mostly choose compassionate people with over-the-top kindness.

Early signs that your partner might be a narcissist:

1. He/she interrupts you when you speak.

2. He/she has a habit of breaking the rules or violating social norms (for example, they might cut in line, treat waiters poorly, often disobey traffic laws and so on).

3. They are always overly attentive with their appearance and take pleasure in making others jealous.

4. Inability to apologize or will feign it and not truly mean it.

5. Inability to take responsibility for their actions. Will resort to 'playing the victim' in arguments and moments of conflict. Nothing is ever their fault.

6. Speaking about themselves in very high terms and comparing themselves to heroes/celebrities/successful people.

7. Having high expectations for you to satisfy their needs.

8. Has the habit of borrowing things or money without returning them.

9. Might push you to overstep personal boundaries.

10. He/she has a very hot and cold personality in your relationship; being overly affectionate/flattering whenever he/she needs something from you and ignoring you when you fail to meet their needs/try to hold them responsible for their actions/words.

11. He/she overreacts because he/she can't distinguish between small events and important issues. The smallest

things can lead to a bombastic reaction.

12. He/she is always right, no matter what. Their views and opinions are the only ones that matter to them.

13. He/she expects you to do whatever they ask you to, without questioning them or hesitating.

14. They use threats a lot, most of them falling either into "I'll break up with you" category or "I will ruin your reputation" category.

15. They make you feel guilty about your actions/decisions, often in situations where there is nothing to feel guilty of.

To recap, relationships with narcissists start on very good terms, as they trick you into believing that you have found the one. This is when they have their "mask" on. The first few weeks/months will be amazing, exciting, passionate, and it will make you deeply love and care for them. By the time they start showing their true colors and "letting the mask slip", it's too late to avoid the abuse that follows. Your brain will refuse to accept the new reality. You will cling and hold on dearly to the initial person you met and the amazing emotions you felt in the beginning.

They will begin using you as their supplier for love, admiration, monetary needs, and whatever desires they will have. Any refusal or critique to the narcissist will be taken as a personal attack (narcissistic injury) and will prompt a bombastic reaction, that will fizzle out as quickly as it started. On an emotional level, the relationship is completely one-sided, you being the only one that loves and cares for him/her.

If you believe that you might be in a narcissistic relationship and you want to break the cycle of abuse, your only option is cutting them from your life, no matter how hard that might be. Later on, in this book, we will talk about advice and strategies to escape from an abusive relationship.

If you already managed to get free of the narcissist's influence, but you have no idea how to regain control over your own life and heal from the abuse, hang tight. We will discuss this later in the book, so don't lose hope. The healing process might be long, and it will take a lot of effort, but in the end, you will get back your happiness and leave this part of your life behind.

In any situation you might be, one thing will never change: relationships with narcissists aren't healthy, and they will destroy you, especially on an emotional level. They are manipulators and abusers by nature, and it's very hard for a person that suffers from NPD to change. Therapy may or may not help them regain some of that humanity they lost, but they first have to acknowledge the fact that they need help. That they are not fine. Since that recognition would put a big hole in their illusion of grandiosity, it doesn't happen that much, and when it does, it's on their own accord. "Fixing them" is not something you can do.

Your only options are: staying in that abusive relationship or escaping from it and taking back control over your life. And only one of them will truly make you happy.

The Birth of a Narcissist

Narcissism usually has roots in early childhood, but it often starts manifesting in a person's teen years and early adulthood. It is widely believed that children who have been victims of abuse, neglect, or otherwise faulty parenting will grow up to display narcissistic behavior, while research is still carried on regarding a possible genetic predisposition to developing NPD. Recent evidence shows that biochemical factors are also to be taken into consideration regarding the origin of narcissism. Highly sensitive people also have a somewhat higher risk of developing NPD as an unhealthy coping mechanism.

Let's start with childhood. Being selfish is part of an infant's development, as it ensures that their immediate needs, such as hunger, are being met. A young child does not have the capacity to understand someone else's feelings or needs, so its focus stays on their own existence. For the child to develop properly and become a functional member of society, this selfishness needs to decline gradually. The child needs to learn how to see life from someone else's perspective and start paying attention to the needs and feelings of others - the basis of empathy. If there is no emotional development, or if the child grows up believing that being vulnerable is not acceptable, then it automatically has a higher risk of being a narcissist in the future. However, clinicians believe that NPD can't be, and shouldn't be diagnosed in children, as it would be incongruent.

Parenting styles that could lead to the creation of a narcissist include: neglecting, setting very high expectations for them, cold/insensitive, overly indulgent, promoting an entitled attitude, and overly controlling.

Trauma and abuse are also two factors that can't be ignored, as they are influential psychological factors. Children, pre-teens, and teens that go through traumatic events or any abuse will have a higher risk of developing bad coping mechanisms or planting the seeds for narcissism, compared to young adults or adults. Even death in the family can be the start of a warped way of dealing with reality if the child doesn't have a positive example to follow or someone to guide him/her through it. Remember that for narcissism, the origins are usually in early childhood, although it can be clinically diagnosed only after the age of 18.

Teenagers, for example, tend to be self-centered, as they are in a confusing time of their lives where they feel the need to be independent. So, it's harder to tell if they are displaying potential narcissistic tendencies or if they are just being rebellious. But there are some red flags that one could notice, even in this early stage of creation of a possible narcissist, such as:

- Overly competitive, to the point that the teen does not mind hurting others as long as he/she wins.

- Lying to get their way/lying whenever it is beneficial for them to lie - without taking responsibility for it.

- Never taking responsibility for their actions/words and blaming others.

- Egotistical to the point where they only care about their themselves and getting their needs catered to, above anyone else's.

- A sense of entitlement that has no real basis other than the fact that they believe they should be treated specially.

- Having bully tendencies to the extent of becoming

verbally abusive/diminishing people with their words.

- Overreacting to criticism, even when it is constructive.

So, after the seed is planted, and we have a mind that doesn't know how to process emotions or how to understand people, what happens? How is a narcissistic mind built? How does it process the world?

After a traumatic event happens in early childhood, the child develops negative feelings, such as shame, towards their "real self." To combat that, this "real self" is buried deep down, and the child suffers from arrested development of their emotional intelligence, keeping emotions such as love, compassion, or their full capacity to feel empathy, severely underdeveloped. Besides relinquishing this "real self" and in order to cope, the child creates a "false self," a mask created by mimicking other people's way of acting that the child finds admirable.

This "split personality" of theirs makes it very hard to spot the narcissist. They can publicly act like regular members of society while in private they abuse and mistreat anyone close to them. Protecting their real self by nurturing and maintaining their false self is the fundament and basis of the narcissist's behavior. To achieve that, a narcissist needs constant reassurance and admiration, which are also called "narcissistic supplies." They depend on these supplies and will do anything to get them, by using manipulation tactics, lies, and abuse. Any critique will remind them of the real self they are hiding, causing hostile defensive responses.

The real self has the following characteristics:

- Buried deep inside their psyche.

- Bears feelings of extreme self-loathing, shame, misery, jealousy of "normal people."

- Desperate protection from being exposed to the world.

- Abusing the people closest to them, the narcissist escapes momentarily from having to deal with their real self.

- Completely passive/paralyzed, has no active role in the conscious mind of the narcissist - making psychotherapy treatment very challenging.

The false self is characterized as:

- A mask/camouflage to hide the real self.

- A shield for the real self.

- Confident, charming, charismatic.

- Rude/impolite to those that he/she believes to be beneath them.

- Prone to explosions of anger - narcissistic fury, and hostility if critiqued - although they pass as fast as they come; when the narcissist feels threatened, we say that he/she suffers a "narcissistic injury."

- Manipulative - knows exactly how to get the attention of a wide variety of people.

- Having a wide circle of people, they know, but no deep relationships - everything is superficial.

- Pathological liar.

Between these two sides of the same coin, there is no competition regarding "who takes control." The real self depends on the false self to survive and cope with reality. Without the presence of the false self, the true self is in danger of disappearing and "dying." By developing this false self, a child becomes immune to the abuse/trauma that it's been through. It shields the true self from pain, and negative emotions, while also actively "hiding" it from the outside world. For the narcissist, their only "self" is the "false self," as it allows him/her to be a "better" version of themselves, one that deserves to be treated better. Although, in essence, this false self starts as a reaction to the abuse/trauma, or a way to adapt to an unhappy life, it ends up being the predominant "self," suffocating the true self and making emotional and personal growth impossible.

The fact that there is a true self, which is weak, underdeveloped, and crippled, and a false self which dominates the psyche of the narcissist, is pretty straightforward and easy to understand. What's harder to pinpoint is how connected these two halves are? Exactly what behaviors can be attributed to which and are there interchangeable? Can the false self "borrow" from the true self's personality in order to fool the world?

The reality is that there are different degrees of "narcissism." A spectrum that goes from milder cases to extremely severe ones. Some narcissists might still show, from time to time, glimpses of his/her true self, meaning that it is not completely passive. However, these cases are fairly rare, and most narcissists simply create a false self that imitates their true selves. Nevertheless, we can go further and settle on two main types of narcissists: The grandiose narcissist and the vulnerable narcissist. These two types originate from different types of childhood experiences, and they manifest in contradictory ways.

The grandiose narcissists are the result of growing up as an entitled kid, who was overly spoiled and was led to believe that he or she was superior and better than the other kids. This type of narcissist tends to be more dominant, aggressive, and very open to telling people how great they are. In relationships, grandiose narcissists are prone to cheating and abruptly leaving their partners when their needs are no longer satisfied.

The vulnerable narcissists are more aware of the illusory aspect of their grandiosity, and they have frequent mood swings. This type of narcissism is usually the result of trauma or neglect, and they feel victimized or attacked whenever things don't go their way. Although they are more sensitive than the grandiose narcissists, they still lack any sort of empathy, and they become dependent on their partners to offer constant supplies to feed their illusions. In a relationship, the vulnerable narcissist will often doubt the sincerity and faithfulness of their partners, while also showing increasing levels of possessiveness and jealousy.

Regardless of the exact type of narcissist, you're dealing with, they all function on the same "true self - false self" system.

How does the false self work? The narcissist employs two mechanisms: re-interpretation and emulation. Re-interpretation is the act of taking emotions and reactions in a positive light. To be more precise, any emotion or reaction that the narcissist does not consider to be socially acceptable or good are warped into something else. Fear, for example, turns into compassion, because that is a feeling that will earn him/her admiration while fear is considered humiliating. By re-interpreting, the narcissist keeps its false self thriving, feeding the illusion of moral superiority.

Emulation is completely different, although the purpose it serves is ultimately the same. While narcissists do not feel or understand empathy, they excel when it comes to simulating emotions. They are first-class observers of human behavior, and they know exactly how to act in certain situations, in order to give the illusion of empathy. This is used to get under their victim's skin and annihilate their natural defenses. They have the ability to get in someone's mind, and they use it to fulfill their need for control and reassurance. In other words, by emulating emotions and empathy, they hook their victims, ensuring a constant supply of whatever they desire, be it admiration, praise, monetary gains, or other types of favors.

Whether we like to admit it or not, narcissists were originally victims, that, in the absence of any guidance and help, built up their own way of dealing with things. One that ended up being toxic for everyone, including the narcissist. Narcissists should be pitied as much as feared because, at the end of the day, they will never know true happiness. Their life is a drama show, created to fool others. They depend on the admiration of their audience. That being said, that doesn't make the narcissist a humanitarian because you should not take it upon yourself to fix him or her. Even specialists have a hard time helping them, and that would also require the narcissist to admit that he or she needs help - which does not happen often. After heavily depending on the false-mask for so long, it is extremely difficult for the narcissist to work towards killing the false-self and developing the real self.

No matter how hard it might be to accept, the narcissist only sees you as supply, an object to be used, and nothing more, and while you are still offering up what he/she needs, the abuse will never stop. Being abusive is their second nature. They can't help it, but you can put an end to it. Leaving an abuser is the first step towards a better life. Your happiness matters!

Unfortunately, a particular group of people with loving and admirable traits get sucked into the narcissist's reality. When these types of people fall in love with a narcissist, it is usually a very long, painful nightmare. Accepting the reality that the narcissist cannot be fixed is challenging, and in most cases, a reality where the victim's beautiful qualities and self-worth are scooped out over time. I know this sounds daunting and depressing right now but have hope. There is light at the end of the tunnel.

In the next chapter, we will look into what exactly these qualities are that narcissists are attracted to when looking for their next victim.

How Narcissists Choose Their Victims

When faced with a skillful emotional predator, most of us would be vulnerable, simply because we are humans. However, narcissists, much like other types of predators, have their preferences. Some traits will make you more likely to be the victim of a narcissist. That being said, it does not mean that the personality traits we are about to go through, are bad or somewhat wrong. In the context of a healthy relationship, these traits would provide the perfect basis for positive developments and growth for both partners. There is no need for you to feel bad about having these traits. But you do have to be wary of the type of people that will be drawn to you, and how they use these traits against you for their own advantage, so you can protect yourself in the future.

Let's see what a narcissist looks for in a person. Maybe this will answer the inevitable question that you probably asked yourself a million times before: "Why me?"

Empathy

The trait that narcissists love the most in their victims. Empathy mixed with deep emotions of love makes for an easy target to manipulate from the narcissist's perspective. Although narcissists themselves are not capable of being empathetic, it is crucial for their survival to target people that have a great deal of empathy. An empathic partner gives the narcissist the emotional fuel it needs to keep his or her false perception of themselves alive.

An empathic person will offer everything in a relationship and will always try to see the situation from the other's perspective, something that facilitates the narcissistic abuse cycle.

This otherwise empowering ability to understand other people's feelings turns into a double-edged sword in the hands of a narcissist. They know that, with such a person, playing victim is a breeze. They will always have an audience for their self-directed and written "drama." They know that they will be forgiven, no matter how much their words/actions have hurt you, and thus, they will never have to take any responsibility.

An empathic person will also hesitate to hold their partners accountable or expose their bad behavior to the world. They feel somewhat compelled to protect their abusers and forgive them, out of a strong sense of guilt. Narcissists know that an empathic person will always put their needs first, making them easy to use tools in their quest of getting what they want/believe they deserve. Also, the forgiving nature of an empathic person makes them more likely to return to an abusive relationship. Empaths are generally kind-hearted individuals that are focused on making the people in their life happy, so we can say they are often "people pleasers." But something else that the narcissist can benefit from is the empath's inability to draw a line. They often have weak boundaries, out of love for their partner and out of a lack of self-worth, which is why they constantly accept/do things they might not be comfortable with.

Long story short: high empathy equals high chances of becoming the target of a narcissist.

This is why we see a lot of Narcissists dating Empaths. You may even be an Empath.

Perfectionism

It may sound weird, but narcissists like to go for people that are extreme perfectionists. These types of people are never satisfied with what they do/achieve, and they genuinely believe there is always room for improvement. A narcissist knows how to use this personality trait in his/her favor. It's a lot easier to convince a perfectionist, that always seeks to please others and that's forever doubtful of everything they do, that they are not good enough. Narcissists will use this insecurity and desire of acknowledgment as a weapon against their partner, especially in the devaluation stage of the relationship.

A perfectionist will always diminish their worth and the importance/quality of their work. For a narcissist, that's extremely convenient.

Conscientiousness

A conscientious person always thinks about what's best for the people around them, and they have the habit of keeping their promises and taking responsibility for their actions. Unfortunately, such people also tend to make the mistake of projecting their idea of morality on others, which will leave them under the false impression that the narcissist will do the same.

A narcissist knows that a conscientious person is one that can be exploited, as they are very likely to offer second chances, will be generally forgiving, and will have a hard time believing that their romantic partner is not as good of a person as they initially thought. Conscientious people also know that in order for a relationship to work, both members have responsibilities and obligations, and often, they will give way and compromise their own happiness in order to please their partners.

Dr. George Simon, an author that's very interested in the ins and outs of narcissistic manipulation, sheds more light onto why conscientiousness is one of the most crucial traits that attract narcissists:

"Disturbed characters most often target folks possessing two qualities they don't possess: *conscientiousness* and *excessive agreeableness* (i.e. deference). So, it's a solid conscience that makes you most vulnerable to narcissistic manipulation. Manipulators use guilt and shame as their prime weapons. But you have to have the capacity for shame and guilt for the tactics to work. Disturbed characters lack that capacity. Conscientious folks have it in spades.

A narcissist might complain about how unfair you are. And because you inherently want to be fair, you take the complaint seriously. It might not occur to you that guilting or shaming you in this way is a tactic. You realize it later when they've taken advantage too many times.

Always having to be "right" pretty much defines narcissistic pride. Conscientious people care about right and wrong. And they don't like being in the wrong. So, all the narcissist has to do is to point out legitimate weaknesses, shortcomings, inconsistencies, minor errors, or missteps. Before you know it, you start seeing things their way. And worse, once you do, you're at greater risk to *defer*."

Intelligence

Narcissists look for people with an above-average intelligence, which are highly skilled and passionate about their careers. Why? Because, in the initial phase of the relationship, the partner is used as an "accessory" to add up to the narcissist's sense of superiority. They take pride in showing their partners off and being associated with them, as long as they remain the main focus of attention.

It may seem contra-productive for a narcissist to go for someone that will sooner or later threaten their sense of superiority, but the truth is that they take pleasure in putting down bright, passionate individuals. In a way, they get to share your spotlight while it lasts and then slowly take away all of your confidence and self-worth, which is a two-in-one package for narcissists.

Integrity

Individuals with integrity are very attractive to narcissists as they offer a lot of opportunities for exploitation. A person with integrity will most likely feel strongly against breaking off a relationship that they have invested in, even if the said relationship is not a positive one. They are open to forgiving their partners, and they don't like to get confrontational. They are very aware of the obligations that a relationship entrails, and they will compromise and try to alleviate conflicts, even if that means giving in.

A narcissist takes all these positive aspects of having integrity and turns them into ways of exploiting and chipping away at the self-trust of their partners. Their strong sense of morality becomes the shackles that keep the abusive relationship going until the narcissist puts an end to it.

Low Self-Esteem and Confidence

Insecurities are part of being human, and narcissists themselves are incredibly fragile when it comes to their perception of themselves. They fight to the death to protect their inflated sense of self. It comes as a logical choice for them to go after people who have self-esteem and confidence issues. Firstly, because they will respond very well to the initial phase of the relationship in which the narcissist "love bombs" its victim. People with insecurities crave compliments and acknowledgment, and the narcissist is more than prepared to deliver.

Secondly, a person that already has issues with how they perceive themselves will be much easier to take apart once the idealization is over. Narcissists have this malicious pleasure to diminish others. The more ammunition they have to accomplish that, the better. In a relationship with a narcissist, your insecurities will always be used against you.

Sentimentality

A sentimental person that's prone to romanticizing a relationship is, perhaps, one of the narcissist's favorite targets. Don't forget that narcissists dedicate the beginning of the relationship to making you feel special and catering to your needs. By doing that, they give a sentimental person, nice memories to cherish and feed on when they start showing their true colors.

Narcissists enjoy games, and they excel at playing with their partner's emotions. They know exactly what they need to say or do, to fabricate that "soulmate" feeling that will make their victims addicted to them, in a deep emotional way. Sentimental people are easy to pick up because they already have that native desire for meaningful human connection - something that a narcissist can mimic effortlessly.

Dr. Paul Babiak and Dr. Robert Hare talk about the way in which a predator assesses their victim and how they are able to fake a genuine bond. Although their book, *"Snakes in Suits: When Psychopaths Go to Work,"* focuses on psychopathic individuals, the next excerpt, from the chapter *Forging the Psychopathic Bond*, offers a very good understanding on how a sentimental person can be manipulated by emotional predators:

"As interaction with you proceeds, the psychopath carefully assesses your persona. Your persona gives the psychopath a picture of the traits and characteristics you value in yourself. Your persona may also reveal, to an astute observer, insecurities or weaknesses you wish to minimize or hide from view. As an ardent student of human behavior, the psychopath will then gently test the inner strengths and needs that are part of your private self and eventually build a personal relationship with you by communicating (through words and deeds) four important messages.

The first message is that the psychopath likes and values the strengths and talents presented by your persona. In other words, the psychopath positively reinforces your self-presentation, saying, in effect, I like who you are. Reinforcing someone's persona is a simple, yet powerful, influence technique, especially if communicated in a convincing—that is, charming—manner. Unfortunately, many people we deal with in our personal and professional lives are so self-absorbed and narcissistic that they rarely see our persona because of the preoccupation they have with their own. Finding someone who pays attention to us, who appreciates or actually "sees" us, is refreshing; it validates who we are and makes us feel special."

Resilience

Being able to bounce back from adverse situations is generally an incredible strength to possess. Unfortunately, narcissists also like having partners that can sustain a lot of "emotional damage" without leaving them. Survivors of abuse or different types of traumas are known to try hard to make everything right, and narcissists get a lot of benefits by being into a relationship with these types of people.

Their "savior syndrome" makes them fight for the relationship and try to "heal" their narcissistic partner, even if, deep inside they know that it's in vain. They get attached to toxic individuals and, what's worse is that they may even equal the amount of abuse they are put through with how much the other person must love them.

A narcissist will almost have an unlimited source of "narcissistic supplies" from a resilient person, as, no matter the amount of pain and abuse, they are very likely to stick around and jump immediately back into the relationship whenever the narcissist hoovers them.

A resilient person that has already been through trauma and abuse is also more prone to getting hooked on small gestures of affection, becoming effectively addicted to the other person. Dr. Joseph Carver, a clinical psychologist, explains in more detail how sporadic acts of kindness can trick resilient people into falling victims of the narcissist's abuse. Dr. Carver focuses on how that manipulation method is used by abusers to "trick" victims of

Stockholm Syndrome, but the information is still relevant regardless of the type of abuse the victim has sustained.

"When an abuser/controller shows the victim some small kindness, even though it is to the abusers benefit as well, the victim interprets that small kindness as a positive trait of the captor... Abusers and controllers are often given positive credit for not abusing their partner, when the partner would have normally been subjected to verbal or physical abuse in a certain situation... Sympathy may develop toward the abuser, and we often hear the victim of Stockholm Syndrome defending their abuser with 'I know he fractured my jaw and ribs... but he's troubled. He had a rough childhood!'

Similar to the small kindness perception is the perception of a 'soft side.' During the relationship, the abuser/controller may share information about their past – how they were mistreated, abused, neglected, or wronged. The victim begins to feel the abuser/controller may be capable of fixing their behavior or worse yet, that they (abuser) may also be a 'victim.'

The admission is a way of denying responsibility for the abuse. While it may be true that the abuser/controller had a difficult upbringing – showing sympathy for his/her history produces no change in their behavior and in fact, prolongs the length of time you will be abused. While 'sad stories' are always included in their apologies–after the abusive/controlling event–their behavior never changes! Keep in mind; once you become hardened to the 'sad stories,' they will simply try another approach."

According to Dr. Carver, manipulators and abusers have learned to shift the blame on a variety of factors from being influenced by violent video games to the extreme of pinpointing "eating too much" as a valid reason for committing murder. They will invent any story if it benefits their exoneration of "bad deeds."

Never trust an abuser's excuses no matter how reasonable they may sound.

Codependency

Leaving these traits aside for a bit, you should also know that people with codependent tendencies are too on the narcissist's "wishlist." Codependency is an emotional and behavioral condition which drastically affects a person's ability to have and maintain a normal, healthy relationship. This type of person always finds themselves in one-sided relationships which are abusive or destructive in nature. A codependent person develops what's known as "relationship addiction" that makes it very hard for them to escape from a toxic partner.

Traditionally, codependency was used to describe relationships with people that struggled with an alcohol or drug addiction. Then the term widened its area of use, after observed similarities of behavior, to also describe relationships with people that have some type of mental illness.

The roots of codependency are established in early childhood. Kids that are part of dysfunctional families are very likely to grow up with codependent tendencies. A dysfunctional family is one in which members suffer from negative emotions (anger, fear, pain, or shame) as a result of a problem that is widely ignored/denied by the said members. What are the most frequent problems hidden under the rug, by members of dysfunctional families? For starters, the existence of abuse, in any shape or form, be it physical, emotional, or even sexual. Then there is the existence of one member who battles some sort of addiction - be it substance abuse or gambling, a toxic relationship, etc. And last but not least, the existence of a family member that suffers from a chronic physical or mental illness.

Because these problems are ignored, family members develop the behavior of repressing their feelings and starting to put the needs of others above their own. That's how most of the resilient people that I have talked about before are born, the so-called "survivors." They learn ways to go around negative emotions, and they fully dedicate themselves to taking care of the person that struggles with addiction/illness, often sacrificing their own needs. These sorts of people can quickly lose sight of what they want and need, overall being prone to struggling with their own identity and sense of self.

Codependent people are characterized by low self-esteem, to the point in which they need something or someone from the outside to latch onto, in order to feel good about themselves. This type of behavior usually ends with some kind of addiction or with the development of compulsive behaviors (like workaholism). In a relationship, a codependent individual has the best intentions but, unknowingly takes on the role of the caretaker, seeking to satisfy the other person's needs. Besides taking care of their partners, they also protect them from having their bad behaviors known to the world and will often make excuses for the way they act in certain situations that may be condemned by others. As the relationship unfolds, the codependent person starts getting a feeling of reward and satisfaction from the fact that they are needed by someone. At some point, they start realizing that they have nothing to say regarding the way the relationship is going but they can't break away from the abuse, addicted to the feeling of validation that the partners give them.

Some characteristics of codependent people include: a sense of responsibility for the actions of others, addiction to relationships in need of validation and to avoid feeling abandoned, lack of trust in their own capabilities, problems with maintaining boundaries, difficulties when it comes to making decisions, a tendency of trying to "save" and "heal" people they are in a relationship with, easily hurt when no one acknowledges their work/effort, and a clear tendency to do more than they need, in any situation.

If you are/were in a relationship with a narcissist/abusive partner, and you were in any way "addicted" to being with that person, that does not automatically make you a codependent individual. You may only have a tendency towards putting your partner's needs above your own and doing your best to keep the relationship alive, despite constant problems. Remember that the narcissist is a first-class manipulator, that knows how to play his/her cards in order to get you hooked and secured. Understand that a victim of narcissistic abuse is very vulnerable and would rather cling to the failed relationship, out of hope for better days, than go back into the dating world. The trust and self-esteem of a victim of narcissistic abuse and their whole image of themselves have been damaged so severely that the simple thought of going back into their lives alone, without a partner to occasionally validate them, is too much to handle. However, if you do believe that you fit the profile of codependency, there are ways to improve your situation, by going to therapy and learn to experience all the emotions repressed due to childhood abuse or having a dysfunctional family.

Empaths

I mentioned this term earlier in the empathy section, and since we're talking about a narcissist's perfect victim, we can't oversee empaths. An empath is a hypersensitive person that can understand and resonate with other people, in a profoundly emotional way. They have the ability of "absorbing" the energies from their environments, good or bad, and they are caring, kind-hearted individuals.

Some traits that characterize an empath are: high sensitivity - they have a lot of heart but are easily hurt, highly intuitive, usually introverts, they have a tendency to absorb the emotions of others, they can get overwhelmed by noise, light, excessive talking or strong smells, they thrive in nature/quiet environments, and they need alone time in order to recharge.

The sensitivity of an empath is both a blessing and a curse. It makes them relate to people uniquely, but it also makes them living targets for energy vampires- such as the narcissist. An energy vampire can easily "eat away" the energy of the empath, leaving them tired and mentally disturbed. On top of that, a narcissist can effortlessly manipulate an empath into believing that they are worthless and undeserving of love.

Emotional vampires are very drawn to empaths because of their compassion and positive energy. They feed on these and thrive, while you are depleted and too tired to care for your wellbeing. If you find yourself in that list of traits listed above, then it's very understandable why you got in this situation. You are like a delicious ice-cream on a hot summer day for your abusive partner.

If you believe you are an empath, and you are able to *feel* the world, then don't fall into despair. There are beautiful things about being an empath. You have the capability to help other people. Also, your feelings and experiences are so intense that they give you a unique view of the world, that few people have. There is a lot of beauty out there, that only an empath can see.

The Cycle of Narcissistic Abuse

A relationship with a narcissist is, and will always be, abusive in nature.

However, what makes it somewhat harder to initially classify it as such is the fact that it does not follow the traditional formula of abuse in domestic situations, which was originally developed by Leonore Walker in 1979. Her model for the cycle of abuse consisted of three main stages: a tension-building stage - when one partner is extremely dominant and overly-demanding while the other complies; the violent episode - the point at which the victim tries to fight back or escape; honeymoon stage - the abuser shows to be remorseful and the victim forgives him/her in hopes of a better future, also this period gives the illusion of a normal relationship.

The cycle of narcissistic abuse has some similarities but, overall, it requires its own "model for domestic abuse" to better fit the situation. The recognized phases and patterns of narcissistic abuse are: Idealize, Devalue, Destroy, Discard, and Hoover.

Idealize

Before the narcissist can start their abuse, they need to entice their victim with positive emotions. This stage marks the beginning of the relationship, where the narcissist "love bombs" their partner and puts him/her on a pedestal. The "love bombing" manifests through excessive compliments, praise, attention, amazing dates, expensive gifts, and it has the purpose of making you feel infatuated and charmed. After some time from all these feel-good emotions, you naturally start to trust the narcissist and feel like you want to open up. Why wouldn't you? You are having such a great time together. When the darker periods of the relationship start to occur later, it is this love-bombing phase that the victim will cling to and try to re-live with their abuser.

By opening up to the narcissist, unknowingly, you start feeding them the data and information they need to get into your mind and find your weak points. Everything you ever told them about your insecurities, past issues, doubts, they will remember and use them as weapons whenever they will want to put you down - in the next stage of abuse.

The way they act during this stage lets their partner believe that they are connecting on a higher level, triggering the "soulmate syndrome" which comes with an extreme emotional link that will be very hard to break. While the victim perceives this idealization stage as the basis and fundamentals for a relationship that's made to last, in the eyes of the narcissist this is nothing more than a game that ensures their next supply.

At the end of this stage, the narcissist begins to see their partner as a "regular human," because of their emotional responses or actions that they do not approve of, and slowly the partner falls off the pedestal.

Devalue

The devaluation stage is characterized mainly by verbal abuse, forms of bullying (humiliation, threats, smearing), and acts of betrayal from the narcissist's side. The relationship jumps from your partner being proud of showing you off and being associated with you to you becoming someone flawed. All of your positive characteristics that he/she has admired before are transformed by the narcissist into something negative. Now you are a smartass instead of intelligent, your confidence is labeled as being cocky - or narcissistic, and your love for yourself and positive body image becomes vanity.

They start to actively put you down and gaslight all of your insecurities by diminishing your worth and your accomplishments. Everything you managed to achieve in life will be diminished, and they will paint your future in a grim light, instilling doubt in your own capabilities and decisions. Blatantly speaking they will do whatever they can to stop you from doing anything that he or she might perceive as an attack on their superiority. At that point, they have their victim trapped in the spider web they created, and they use their power and influence over you to dictate what you should think, your beliefs, your dreams, your image of yourself, your life choices, and the people that should or should not be in your life.

Their control is so powerful that your whole perception on life flips on its head, leaving you traumatized and heartbroken. This verbal abuse and diminishing will not stop until they completely strip you out of your free will, actively destroying you, or better said, the *you* that you knew/were before him.

You need to understand that this phase does not begin as a response to you doing something wrong. The victim bears no fault into the way that the narcissist chooses to interpret their actions or words. And through this whole process, the victim is clueless. They don't understand what they have gotten into, they don't see the web of lies and deceit trapping them. The victim gets so emotionally tired of all the insults and verbal abuse that comes their way that they would do virtually anything to get back to the original phase of the relationship when everything seemed perfect. The partners of narcissists will cling so hard to these memories of a better time, and they will truly believe in their hearts that going back is possible.

Destroy

Meanwhile, the narcissist stays on its road to destroy you and strip you of any ounce of confidence you might still have in your body. They will treat you in a barely acceptable way, putting in the least amount of effort. Even compliments will be used as a double-edged sword that will seek more to hurt you than to soothe your already bleeding heart. By this point, thanks to their manipulation, you already become dependent on them to offer you validation and admiration. As they go on with the devaluation and destroying your very person, they will use this desire of validation that you have against you. Anything you do will be seen as bad, and you will never reach the high standards they set, no matter how hard you try.

Other weapons that the narcissist will use in this stage is accusations and blame-shifting. Whenever the victim tries to defend herself/himself or tries to make the narcissist take responsibility for the way their words affect you, they will flip the situation and make themselves the "victim." They will blame you for being overly-sensitive, not smart enough to understand what they mean. They will emphasize how different you two are, mostly by portraying you as inferior / not worthy of being in a relationship with them. The narcissist will compare its actual victim with his or her ex-conquers, representing them as better in any way that you are. They will accuse you of things that more accurately describe them than you, such as: being self-centered, being a narcissist, not being understanding of their feelings and needs, not doing anything for them.

Out of all the stages that define narcissistic abuse, devalue - destroy is the one that comprises most of the per se abuse. It is done carefully, in a cold and malicious way, as the narcissist uses all the data that he/she has collected from you in the "idealize" stage, in order to break you apart piece by piece. Their only reason for doing that is to feed their illusion of superiority in the only way that he/she can: belittling you. Their whole life purpose is feeling good about themselves, no matter what tactics they need to employ in order to do that, or what/how many people will need to be exploited to achieve that.

Discard

When the victim finally reaches breaking point and has had enough and demands to be treated in a better way, they will discard the victim, in the search for someone new to idealize and repeat the cycle. This can happen quite quickly. Quicker than you expect as the narcissist most likely has had other victims entangled in the web in the early stages without you knowing. Social Media makes it a lot easier for the narcissist to keep multiple partners at bay.

Hoover

If most of the abuse happens in the devalue and destroy stages, this is one that can make the victim go through serious emotional trauma. When a narcissist discards a partner, it's only temporarily. They will most likely return to try and get their ex back into a relationship with them, even if they might already be involved with other people. As long as the narcissist believes that he or she can gain something by having you back, they will do everything in their power to get you back, continuing the cycle of abuse until the victim is strong enough to break it.

The heartbreaking fact is that, even when they are being discarded and forgotten for weeks or months, victims of narcissistic abuse will accept to give the relationship another try. It's not just the fact that they become addicted, but the victim finds it very hard to re-adjust back to their old life without the narcissist. Having parts of their identity stripped away, and their confidence at its lowest point makes going back into the world of dating and meeting new people seem incredibly daunting and scary. The loneliness and depression felt can be so deep, that it's almost impossible to resist when the narcissist attempts to "hoover" them, in the form of a text, call or Facebook message for example. The victim might get back together with the narcissist even if she/he was the one that initiated the break-up, and not the narcissist. That's just how powerful the influence of a person that has NPD is on a person with low confidence and self-worth.

The victim needs to understand that this attempt to get back together does not come out of feelings of love, concern, or the compelling need to re-connect. The narcissist will hoover their victim because they enjoy the feeling of power they get from it. It feeds their ego to know that they can get you back, whenever they want, as it shows how much control and power they have over you. They feel good knowing that they always have a backup supply to come back to, whenever they have needs to be catered to, and they will shamelessly do that even while actively pursuing other people or being in other relationships - especially if that other partner does not supply enough admiration/attention. The victim needs to understand that their relationship with the narcissist was never about love, not in the narcissist's perspective. Their sole purpose for wanting you back is to get something and to feel good about how they can bend people to their will. They don't miss the victim, because they are unable of having such strong feelings. The more people trapped in the narcissist's web, the better for them. Any action they employ is only for their gain and benefit. Love was never and will never be in her/his mind.

Fundamentals of Narcissistic Abuse & Cognitive Dissonance

In both the traditional cycle of abuse and narcissistic abuse, there are stages of rising and falling tension. The period of idealized/perfect relationship ends abruptly after an incident which triggers a violent episode, in traditional abuse cases or the beginning of the devaluation stage, in narcissistic abuse. In the latter case, there are multiple incidents of abuse in the devaluation stage, which will culminate with the narcissist discarding the victim, at least for some time. The moments of falling tension are characterized by the honeymoon period in traditional abuse cycles and by the hoovering in narcissistic abuse. In both models of abuse, the abusers will try to promote positive bonding (for example, the narcissist puts a temporary stop to devaluation and goes back to idealizing its victim) which makes it hard for the victims to escape the relationship. And so, the cycle begins again and repeats itself until the partner of the abuser puts a stop to it.

Christine Hammond, a mental health counselor, proposed a different model for the narcissistic abuse cycle, which focuses on the motivation of the abuser. It serves as a further way to differentiate traditional abuse from narcissistic abuse, and it offers a closer look at the dynamics of a relationship with a narcissist (which is solely driven by the narcissist's needs and desires). Hammond concluded that, at some point in the relationship, the narcissist begins to feel threatened by their partner. Remember that narcissists have very frail egos, and they might feel attacked by words and actions which have no ill-meaning behind them. When the narcissist perceives the "threat," that's when the abuse starts. They then proceed to devalue their partners, all while victimizing themselves, and, by the time the partner is deprived of any positive characteristics, the narcissist goes back to feeling superior/powerful. So, the model of abuse goes as follows: the narcissist feels threatened - the narcissist abuses their partner - the narcissist plays the victim - the narcissist feels superior/empowered.

Hammond's model for narcissistic abuse also highlights the different reasons for which victims go back into the relationship. In traditional abuse cases, the abusers actually experience remorse, and they convince their partners to offer them another chance with promises of change, which triggers the start of another honeymoon period that makes the victim think that the abuse is over. The victims of narcissistic abuse also hope that their partners would revert back to that initial phase of their relationship, but they are "forced" to stay in the relationship by the narcissist's methods of manipulation and victimization. Narcissists experience no genuine feelings of remorse, and their only motivation from getting back a partner is to satisfy their needs further.

In the traditional model of abuse, it has been noted that the abuser actively tries to keep the relationship going, even when the partner is aware of the toxic cycle they are stuck in. Narcissistic partners don't care if the relationship holds or not, and they only "fight" to keep a victim hooked to feel powerful over someone else and to continue using the said person. Also, the victims of narcissistic abuse are rarely aware of the toxic cycle that's part of their relationship. The narcissistic abuser has so much power over its victim that he or she feeds their partner their point of view, shifting the blame and making their partner oversee their wrongdoings. Victims of narcissistic abuse experience a type of "abuse amnesia" in which they forget all the negative feelings and thoughts they had for their abusive partner, a result of the narcissist's manipulation and constant abuse.

Victims of narcissistic abuse also suffer from cognitive dissonance. Most people require their behaviors and beliefs to be consistent. When a belief has been held firmly for quite some time, and then new evidence challenges this belief, it causes disharmony and great pain. The longer the belief has been held, the harder it can be to break. The victim can either choose to 'turn a blind eye' to this new evidence, holding onto the original belief OR respect the new evidence, break the initial belief and accept the pain to their identity.

In the first months of the relationship, the victim is so impressed and infatuated with the narcissist, utterly unaware that the emotions they are developing, are to a false identity; A mask. After some time, when the phases of devaluation and discard begin, and the mask slips off, it is hard for the victim to respect this new piece of evidence. It is much easier for the victim to continue believing in the false narrative holding onto the good emotions felt in the idealize phase rather than acknowledging the new evidence and change of behavior from their partner.

Acknowledging the reality that you fell in love with a 'person' that does not exist is excruciatingly painful. It can take many years for the victim to finally accept this as a reality, and in some unfortunate cases, the victim will refuse to accept this completely. During the cycle of abuse, the victim is continuously in a state of hope that their relationship will revert back to those 'perfect days,' replaying the positive shared moments experienced in their head. This, along with the fact that they are tricked into feeling responsible for the failed relationship, makes it very hard for the victims of narcissistic abuse to officially escape, prompting them to accept the narcissist back into their lives whenever he or she is hoovering them.

Main ideas about narcissistic abuse:

- It is preceded by a period in which the relationship is exciting/perfect.
- It starts when the narcissist perceives something that the victim did/said as a threat.
- The partner of a narcissist has no fault in triggering the abuse as narcissists have a warped way of perceiving reality, and the tendency of making everything personal.
- The narcissist uses manipulation to make themselves the victim of any situation that might put them in a bad light.
- The forms of abuse a narcissist will employ are: verbal, mental, and emotional.
- A narcissist will discard their partners whenever they feel that they are fighting back or when they no longer receive the admiration/love/monetary gain/sexual services they require.
- A relationship with a narcissist is never truly over after a break-up. The abuser will try to come back either to make themselves feel empowered by the control they have over you or because their new supply is not satisfying all their needs.
- Victims of narcissistic abuse have a hard time escaping the relationship because the reality of falling in

love with a false identity is too painful to accept. Their confidence and self-worth is depleted; they feel guilty about the break-up, they are prone to forgetting and overlooking the abusive episodes/negative characteristics of their narcissistic partner; and co-dependent tendencies make it very difficult to fight off this addiction when the narcissist keeps trying to get back into their lives.

- A narcissist never misses their ex-partners, and they don't feel remorse for their actions. The only reason they try to get back into a relationship is to continue using that person to satisfy their needs. In a narcissist's heart, there is no room for love.

The Narcissists Arsenal

A narcissist has many weapons in their arsenal when it comes to getting what they want out of a relationship.

Love bombing

Something that we have already touched on before. Love bombing is the first weapon that they use to 'reel you in.' Love bombing consists of a persistent wave of compliments, flattering comments, material proofs of affection, kind gestures, and touching. All this "show" that they make out how much they adore you has the sole purpose of making you believe that you may have found an amazing partner for a serious relationship. It may feel intoxicating in a good way, and, for people that have struggles maintaining a positive image of themselves and are co-dependent, it will offer a much-needed validation of their worth. Through love bombing, they manage to manipulate you not only into having romantic feelings for them but also to spend more time in their company, depriving you of your alone time or time that you'd typically spend with friends and family.

A narcissist will also be persistent in reminding you how "perfect you are for each other," and it's only thanks to their unusual charm that you are unable to see how weird that may be to say at the start of a relationship where you don't really know your partner that well. Love bombing basically serves the purpose of getting you where the narcissist wants: isolated from friends/family, in love with a charming "persona" that they manufactured to mirror your needs and beliefs, and forced into a relationship that's moving way too fast but unable to realize how smothering this sort of behavior is.

Manipulation

Narcissists will use multiple forms of manipulation. They know how to find your insecurities early on and then use them to gaslight you in the "devalue" stage. They victimize themselves always, feigning innocence at all costs, no matter how many lies they have to serve you or how much they need to distort the truth in order to get out of a sticky situation. Denial is in their DNA, so, whenever they are responsible for any bad situation, they will go to the moon and back to try and make you believe their perspective, never willing to accept the consequences of their actions/words.

Arguments and fights are also used by the narcissist to showcase his/her abilities to play victim, all while actively blaming you and diminishing you for things that they are actually guilty of. They will deny and repeatedly lie to keep alive the illusion of innocence, even when you confront them with solid evidence. Even at times when they might slip the mask a bit and show their true character, they will still be persistent in their trials of having you give them the benefit of the doubt, and thus, spinning the situation in their favor. It "helps" a lot that their partners are kind-hearted individuals that over-estimate the good in people and have the tendency of overlooking their negative traits.

But why do they employ the use of fights and arguments? Logically speaking, couldn't that lead to a potential break-up if they go too far? Well, yes and no. Narcissists love to play with the mind and feelings of their partners. They take pleasure in getting any sort of reaction because in that way they get to suck out your energy (FYI: narcissists are frequently called energetic vampires) and, as a side-effect, they get to test how much power and influence they have over you. The fights will always start as a result of something that the narcissist did/said, and they will always end with the partner taking the blame/forgiving them. Either way, they will benefit both from stealing away your emotional energy and from playing around with your mind - something that helps them keep the illusion of superiority alive.

Projection

Another weapon that is often used by your regular narcissist is projection. It's a very peculiar and strange thing to employ if you take some time to consider it, as projection ultimately shows the flaws and bad side of the narcissist. In a way, by using projection, they "betray" their cover. In simple terms, projection is a defensive mechanism that is characterized by accusing others of something that you are/have done. This is very apparent during arguments or fights when the narcissist will place on you all the bad/negative characteristics that they have or any bad actions that they did or would do, even if those could never truly characterize you. They basically take all of the emotions, characteristic traits, thoughts, flaws that they have and are not comfortable with, and they "give" them to you, so *they* won't be forced to deal with them.

Narcissists are unable to take responsibility for anything, so it is in their nature to shift the blame onto someone else. That's what projection is: a combination of blame-shifting and misdirecting feelings/thoughts. Instead of accepting them as their own, they reflect them on others to protect their frail grandiose image of themselves. They are also managing to distract you from seeing the truth, and they make you claim responsibility for something that they are guilty of. Good examples of projection are the narcissist being overly jealous and convinced that you might be cheating on them, all the while they are the ones that are seeing other people behind your back. Or the narcissist might badmouth someone and critique them for the way they look or for a character trait that they also possess. For narcissists, projection is crucial for their survival, as it allows them to assess their negative feelings/traits/habits without having to actively deal with them or accept them, protecting their false self from harm.

Language

Now let's speak about language and communication. Even those are not safe from the corruption of a narcissistic individual. It becomes a full-blown weapon of war made to protect themselves at all costs and used to harm others. They use communication merely as a way to deceive, hide, and evade blame, but they don't actually transmit any messages. They have strangely mastered the art of speaking a lot without saying anything - something they will mainly use to monopolize conversations or confuse partners when they confront them with evidence of misconduct. Language serves the purpose of belittling others and keeping a narcissistic supply nearby. They never use it to speak *to* people, but rather to speak *at* them, lecturing them on senseless subjects and camouflaging their own vile character. The way that a narcissist uses language is almost impossible to understand as it makes no sense.

Shmuel Vaknin, the author of "Malignant Self Love: Narcissism Revisited," does an excellent job of describing how a narcissist uses language. Let's take a normal conversation for a second. We, as human beings, tend to communicate with one another by transmitting information. This information may be right or wrong, subjective or objective, emotional or scientifical, that does not matter. The core of communication is *transmitting*, in order to potentially build relationships or just for the sake of human contact.

In this aspect, narcissists are very different from regular people. They don't use communication as a means of transmitting anything. The information they blast is empty of any substance. For them, language is just a weapon of manipulation, a means to defend themselves against critiques or opinions that differ from their own or a way to critique/diminish others. Agreements or commitments mean nothing more than a momentary intent to a narcissist.

The narcissist will often lose himself/herself in loop-hole type conversations, where they say the same things all over again, and they often contradict themselves although they seem blissfully unaware of that discrepancy. Many of their statements will defy logic and reality, and any attempt at correcting them will get their conversation partners nowhere. Logic and consistency simply do not define the conversation pattern of a narcissist.

So what are the elements to look for in a conversation with a potential narcissist?

- statements that defy logic/reality
- repetition
- sentences that remain unfinished
- saying a lot without actually saying anything
- a one-sided show that resembles a preach or speech

more than a conversation

Shmuel Vatkin also focuses on the fact that narcissists will generally avoid any serious or meaningful conversation, preferring to play out their own fake narrative in their minds in which everyone adores them. Instead of seeing people as they really are, they will create projections of them, who, in their mind, are made to serve him or her and cater to his or her needs. Whenever the narcissist gets into a situation in which the real person does not comply with his/her mental image of them, he/she will be very surprised and will refuse to accept reality. For example, the narcissist might word his/her surprise over the fact that his/her son did not follow them as an example, as a matter of choosing careers, not being aware that the child in question never had any intention to do so. Or the narcissist might say that his wife changed and no longer listens to him, not realizing the fact that she only did so out of the fear/desire to save the relationship, not because she adored him.

If we are to believe Shmuel Vatkin, a conversation with a narcissist is never a real option, because you can't communicate if both parties are not interested in doing so. A conversation will always be just a one-sided act, in which the truth will most likely be distorted.

Cognitive dissonance

Last but not least, in our list of the weapons that a narcissist uses/relies on, we have cognitive dissonance. I've mentioned it briefly before, but now we are going to go a little bit deeper into it and see how that aids the narcissist in his/her quest to brainwash their victims. The idea behind cognitive dissonance is that, whenever we are faced with something that is not consistent with what we believe or when we are confronted with new information regarding something that we feel strongly about, we unconsciously find a psychological way in which we make said thing seem consistent. The most striking examples of that are apocalyptic type cults or conspiracy theorists that will keep on believing something despite an incredible amount of factual evidence against it.

Now, cognitive dissonance is a frequent normal phenomenon that we all have to deal with on a daily basis, whenever we are faced with information that may question something that we believe/think highly of. Because this is an unconscious phenomenon, we will meet people that are very careful with their health but indulge in bad behaviors such as drinking or consuming dangerous substances, or people that always boast about needing to save money despite them buying useless things on a regular basis.

When we add a narcissist into the mix, cognitive dissonance goes to a whole new level. The narcissist will constantly force their partners to go over the information and choose what to believe. They are fully aware of how difficult it may be to have two separate images of them: the charming person from the beginning of the relationship and the selfish partner. And they use this "discomfort" to get their way. When a person has cognitive dissonance, their initial beliefs regarding their partner are very resistant to change as they have developed a plethora of secondary beliefs on top of them, which basically comprises the way they have been living their lives. This foundation is so strong that it would take a lot of psychological effort to change it and accept a conflictual view. For people that are in relationships with narcissists, they form this strong belief in the first stage of the relationship. They become fully convinced that their partner is "the one," and no matter how much their partner changes and how far he/she goes from their original "persona," the victim will constantly hold onto this belief that there must be an explanation for the strange behavior. In other words, they will find excuses or reasons, no matter how illogical they might seem, in order to keep that initial belief, that they have a good person next to them, intact.

Bree Bonchany, a therapist that works with victims of narcissistic abuse, explains how this initial belief forms, and how victims cling to it, despite constant proof that their partner is not who they thought:

"The love-bombing of the idealization stage of a toxic relationship sows the initial seeds of cognitive dissonance. The narcissist fakes being the ideal partner by saying and doing all the right things. They pretend to be everything we ever dreamed of and shower us with promises of perfect and eternal love. We are conned into believing the narcissist is the best partner we've ever had and the most wonderful person on the planet. We trust their promises and believe they're able to love wholeheartedly, and without limits, in the same way, we do.

We fall madly in love, and our brains become drenched in a potent cocktail of love-bombing, and the pleasure-inducing chemicals, that are released by neurotransmitters in our brains, when we are in love. This potent cocktail is what germinates the seeds of cognitive dissonance, which were planted in our minds, during the idealization stage.

By the time the devaluation stage occurs, and the narcissist's behavior begins to deviate from the way they first acted, our positive regard for them, and our beliefs about their good character and intentions, have grown like weeds that have permeated, and become firmly rooted throughout our minds."

According to Bonchany, the confusion created by the two opposite beliefs causes mental stress, and we choose to stick to our original beliefs as a way of protecting ourselves because we are not mentally and emotionally ready to accept reality. We do that by denying the new information, finding explanations for it or simply ignoring it. Sometimes we may even take the blame in an effort to protect the relationship, or we actively choose to live "in the past" when the narcissist was still that lovable, charming person - refusing to see the monster he/she has become.

The consequence of this is that the victim suffers a detachment from reality. The inconsistencies in behavior, statements, and beliefs are so severe that the person subjected to them might feel like they're going crazy. Any mentally healthy person is not psychologically prepared to face a relationship with a narcissistic individual. The victims become so brainwashed that she or he starts to actually believe that they do not know how a relationship should be and how it should work, ultimately letting the narcissist take the wheel. Whenever the belief that his/her partner might not be good for them creeps in, a memory of better times will also pop up in their minds, stopping victims of narcissistic abuse from making any definite decision regarding the relationship.

Cognitive dissonance is the worst weapon that a narcissist can use because it has multiple negative effects:

1. It makes the partner develop loyalty towards the narcissist. Also known as 'Stockholm Syndrome.' A condition in which the victim develops a psychological alliance with their captor during captivity.

2. It allows for partners of narcissists to sustain abuse without realizing it.

3. It makes victims of abuse vulnerable to being used

by the narcissist, and it keeps them in a constant state of bad mental health.

4. It has long term effects that will haunt victims of narcissistic abuse a long time after the relationship is over, leaving them unable to understand what has happened to them and prone to getting themselves in similar situations.

I hope this chapter shed some light on how resourceful narcissists are and why it is so easy to fall into their trap and stay there. Understanding what you were/are up against is one of the first steps towards escaping and rediscovering yourself.

Narcissist's Language

Narcissists are skilled manipulators, and part of that is thanks to their ability to play with words and their meanings. To really get a grasp on how the mind of a narcissist works, you need to understand their language. Nothing is as it seems. So, let's look at some usual phrases and see what the actual message behind a narcissist's compliments, apologies, and overall speech is.

Compliments

"You are so much better than my ex. He/she was crazy!" - "In reality, it is my fault that we broke up, I was the problem. But you don't need to find that out, because I'm never guilty of anything. If you leave me or we break up, I'll say the same about you."

"You are my soulmate." - "You are my target right now, and I'll say anything to get you to like me. I'll keep love bombing you with compliments until you give up and accept me in your life."

Apologies

"Sorry you feel that way." - "I don't believe there is any reason for me to apologize, but I will do it to shut you up. I am never wrong / I can never do anything wrong. It's always your fault for being a normal person and displaying emotions / reacting to my abusive behavior."

**"It's not going to happen again / I promise not to do it

again." - "I will absolutely repeat this action/behavior that upset you. If you catch me in the act again, I'll lie and come up with excuses, just to keep this relationship going a little longer. Never believe my promises."

Complaints

"**You are so emotional/dramatic/sensitive/insecure**." - "I need you to think that your way of behaving is wrong and that your reactions are over the top, so I can get away with my actions/behavior. In reality, I like to stir up drama and to gaslight your insecurities, to make you more manageable. I am also overly sensitive to criticism, and I will over-react whenever my superiority is being questioned."

"**You take everything too seriously / You have no sense of humor**." - "I use humor as an excuse to insult you and make you feel less of a person. I take pleasure in deliberately hurting you and then pretending that it was all a joke."

"**You're such a smartass/nerd/know it all**." - "You are smarter than me, and I don't like that. I always need to feel superior in any way, and your intelligence threatens me, so I have to make you feel bad for being correct/smart."

"**You never do anything for me!**" - "That's far from the truth, but I want to make you feel like a horrible person, even though I am the one that never does anything for you. I need to feel morally superior to you, so I'll undermine your kindness."

"**We never have sex / My ex loved to (*a sexual act that you are uncomfortable with*), but you never want to try it**." - "I want you to feel bad for not satisfying my every wish and desire. I'm blatantly lying about my ex, in order to get you closer to complying to my every whim. There is a chance that you will feel guilty enough to overstep your boundaries, which no one should be forced to do."

"You are such a narcissistic person / You only think about yourself." - "I want you to feel toxic and guilty in order to put myself in a good light and keep the relationship alive. In this way, I can go on abusing you, without having to answer for my actions. I am the narcissistic one, and I will always put myself first, no matter what. I will do my best to manipulate you into believing that you are the crazy one in this relationship."

Using "break-up talk" as a means of keeping you hooked

"You are too much for me." - "I can't handle your emotions even though I am actively provoking you, any chance I get. Your emotions are annoying to me, and I want you to believe that you're over-reacting."

"We are just so different / We have nothing in common." - "I lack any ability to empathize, and I am not compatible with anyone. But I need you to feel like the problematic one in this relationship. I want you to feel bad for having feelings and human reactions, even though I am the one that affects our relationship."

"Let's take a break." - "I need to make you feel insignificant and to crave my attention while I go about my life finding possible targets and not caring about the pain I'm putting you through. You will want me back anyway."

"I'm done." - "You'll never get away from me. I will always come back when I feel like it. I have no intention of breaking up, but I'm in a situation where you want to make me accountable for my words/actions, and I need to get out of it. I will never take responsibility for my actions/words, and I will find ways to pin the blame on you and make you feel like you or your opinions don't matter. If we ever break up, I will try to get back to you and ruin you as much as I can."

"**Let's just be friends with benefits**." - "A break-up is inevitable, but I still want to have a way of coming back into your life later on and continue my abuse. Or, I know you love me, but I want to lower your expectations while I wait to find someone else."

Manipulative/Controlling phrases

"**My ex would never do that**." - "I want you to feel inferior and to question the way you are acting/reacting. Your behavior is normal, and my ex probably reacted the same, since I'm not with them anymore, but I don't want you to think that you are entitled to acting/reacting that way. You need to feel like the odd one out, the guilty one, so I can get away with my behavior."

"**She/He is just a friend**." - "I need a backup plan to satisfy my needs, be it monetary or sexual, while also making you feel insecure. I feel so powerful knowing that I make you question your worth by having this 'friend.' If things go wrong with you, this 'friend' is my next target."

"**I don't want to have sex with you / I don't care about sex**." - "I want you to feel undesirable and unable to fulfill my desires/fantasies/standards. It will allow me to get away with looking for other sources for sexual gratification. I also enjoy making you feel insecure as it strengthens my power over you."

"**You should be careful with the people you put your trust in**." - "You have people in your life that love and support you, and I don't. I want to ruin your relationship with other people out of sheer jealousy and to further establish my influence over you. The lonelier you are the easier I can manipulate you."

"Nobody cares about you or your accomplishments." - "You need to be dependent on me so I can be the superior one. There are too many people caring about you, and I want you to question their honesty and reasons. I want to isolate you, so you have no support. You only need me."

Narcissists know how to plant the seed of doubt in your brain. They use words as weapons and they will always attempt to diminish you, either by making hurtful jokes or by painting you as the "bad guy." How many of these phrases are familiar to you? Are you able to see the bigger picture now that you have a "translation" of what your partner was actually saying? You can see how these 'digs' at your self worth over a long period of time can really affect you.

The main ideas that you should take away from this chapter are:

1. Never let anyone establish your worth as a human being.

2. In fights/conflicts, guilt is shared between the participants. Always be wary of people that never take responsibility for their actions and constantly play the victim.

3. Don't let anyone disconnect you from your support network. Your friends and family would never think bad of you or judge you.

4. It's perfectly normal to have emotions, that doesn't make you overly sensitive.

5. Maintain your boundaries and never let someone force you out of your comfort zone in any situation, especially in sexual ones.

6. In a healthy relationship, no one is superior. You are equal human beings that work together towards a better future and a happy life. Differences are fine and should be embraced, not used against each other.

7. Excuses and apologies mean nothing if a person is not actively trying to better themselves and not repeat the same mistakes.

Hardships of Escaping an Abusive Relationship

We've talked about what narcissists are, how they choose their victims, how they make you lose control over your life, and how we can characterize narcissistic abuse. But, one more thing needs to be set in stone before we start on the healing journey, and that is how exorbitantly hard it is to escape an abusive relationship.

The world is full of people that share their opinions on sensitive topics without having any factual basis on what they are actually talking about. We live in an era of information, but, ironically, we are more misinformed than ever. Which is why people still ask themselves why men or women that are in abusive relationships don't just leave and never look back? Why are they accepting to be treated badly, and even go as far as to protect their abusers? That is the toxic mentality of blaming the victim, for a situation that is incredibly complex, on a psychological front. And the bad part is that a lot of the victims of narcissistic abuse already blame themselves for the situation they went through and for the failed relationship.

It's enough to just take a look back at one of the previous chapters in this book, "The Narcissists Arsenal," to at least start to understand why victims feel compelled to stay. Narcissists have so many tactics and weapons that they ruthlessly use, and they also know how to choose the perfect targets. They purposely go for people that are very "in tune" with the feelings of others, that have a tendency of putting the needs of others first, that are generally trusting and kind, with low self-esteem and have high traits of co-dependency. It's like using nuclear weapons to take down a rural village full of farmers, with little to no knowledge of wars. Narcissists are predators that feed on other people's energy and emotions. They are first-class manipulators that plan their every move and do whatever it takes to get what they want. How is anyone supposed to be prepared for something like that? For an encounter with a movie-like villain that knows exactly how to get you hooked?

Let's backtrack a little and give a summary of how someone becomes the victim of a narcissist.

The unaware victim is idealized/love-bombed by a charming, well-spoken individual, and ends up falling in love with a mask, an illusory image that the narcissist displays. The abuser keeps up the facade of love and appreciation until they are confident that their partner is fully invested in the relationship - only then the true character of the narcissist starts to show its ugly sight. Many of these victims get into the relationship as strong-willed, independent people, but they are slowly stripped of any positive traits. Their empathy and kindness are used against them, and the constant manipulation tears them apart. The power of the relationship is in the hands of the narcissist, and the love and affection are one-sided. The abuser slowly chips away at their victim's self-worth, exploits them in order to satisfy their own needs and manipulate their way out of any confrontation. The narcissist never feels remorse and avoids any responsibility for his/her actions/words, projecting anything "bad" onto their victims. As the abuse intensifies, the victim starts feeling hopeless. They are always emotionally assaulted, verbally abused, and practically terrorized on a psychological level until they have only a few choices left: to deny the abuse, to minimize its significance, to rationalize the whys behind their partner's behavior, or to find a way to revitalize the relationship and improve their "bond" with the abuser.

I've already dabbled in codependency and how codependent tendencies can trap you in an abusive relationship. But, even in the absence of codependency, the abuse itself has a very traumatizing effect on the brain, which can tie a victim to its abuser, both psychologically and organically (referring to biochemical reactions such as the secretion of neuro stimulants like dopamine and serotonin). This "connection" is known as trauma bonding. No matter how strong-willed a person is or was prior to the relationship, in time, as the abuse escalates, they can show signs of trauma bonding, post-traumatic stress disorder, or complex post-traumatic stress disorder - a prolonged and more extreme version, as a matter of symptomatology, of PTSD. Severe chronic abuse and trauma will have a life-changing effect on anyone, no matter how tough they think themselves to be. And that's an accurate way to describe a relationship with a narcissist: constant severe abuse.

If we are going into the biology of trauma bonding, it all goes back to our inborn need to rely on someone else, for survival. Even after years of evolution, survival still stays at the core of human attachment, which is why we want a partner that makes us feel secure, protected, and cared for. When we find a person that, we believe, can provide what we need, our brains release oxytocin, also known as the "love hormone." We are wired to turn to a person we see as a caretaker (a parent, sibling, friend, partner) whenever we feel threatened by something. But, when the threat (abuser) also happens to be a caretaker figure, trauma bonding develops. Regardless of the abuse, we are unable to stop feeling linked to that person. Whenever the victim starts seeing the contradictions between the actions of their partners (care mixed with abuse) they try their best to rationalize them, which only further strengthens the bond. Especially when the abuser is a narcissist: they know how and when to push your buttons, and they have the tendency of twisting the reality of the victim until it starts seeing things from the abuser's perspective. The bond is also harder to break because of the narcissist's habit of hoovering their victims, whenever they please.

The effects of traumatic bonding vary from obvious to subtle and hardly noticeable. A very general effect of any abuse is the overproduction of cortisol. This hormone that is normally produced whenever we face a stressful situation can be very damaging if it goes over the usual marks. It can cause anxiety, damage the immune system, and negatively impact our blood pressure. Besides hormonal issues, traumatic bonding can also cause depression, sexual dysfunction, PTSD, and a slew of other health issues such as asthma, or fibromyalgia - characterized by muscle pains, fatigue, and mood issues.

There are other factors that make it harder on victims of abuse to break free from their abusers, which are: the inability to perceive that the relationship is toxic, the fear of starting from scratch with another person, the power that the narcissist has over their victims may be close to impossible to overcome, the belief that their partner might change, the misconception that they are in some way responsible for the behavior of their partner, or there might be other things or aspects of their life that link them to the abusers (monetary dependency, having a family with them, etc.).

Ambient abuse can also be put on this list, as it is a subtle, stealthy abuse that the victim most probably won't notice until it's too late. It is considered as one of the most dangerous forms of abuse, especially because of its ambiguous nature.

To end this chapter on an interesting note, here is the perspective of a self-aware narcissist, H.G Tudor, who seeks to help victims understand what has happened to them:

"You fell in love with an illusion. You fell hard and deep for something which never existed. The golden days that we created together were the twisted reflections of my manipulative hold over you. I know how anxious you were to try to recover the golden period. I know that my silence, my verbal violence, the cheating, and the lies, my perfidious control of you was brutal, malicious, and devastating. I understand that the whole avalanche of manipulative techniques I applied to you, in savage wave after wave crushed your self-esteem, mauled your sanity, and shattered your world. This brutality was nothing compared to the aftermath.

For now, you have slipped away from my tight, choking grip.

Memory after memory stirs from within, an endless loop of 'best of' moments that you want to stop remembering but you cannot. It hurts yet you still want to remember because even as the pain rises in your chest, you still feel the flicker of your love for me and you still cherish that.

The one lingering, torturous pain that still sits deep within you is the knowledge that you were in love with an illusion. No matter how much you discuss it with your friends, the earnest hours with your therapist and the pile of books about healing that are stacked up beside your favorite chair, none of them help take away that awful aching.

You can manage the shame of being fooled. You take a strange pride in having given your all to such a despicable person because that is the person you are. Honest, decent and a provider of unconditional love. You do not want that to change. You do not want to lose the empathy for which you are renown.

Your head will eventually accept what happened, that you were charmed, entranced and enchanted and you never stood a chance. That was why you were chosen. Emotionally, you will never lose that dull ache as you sit and reminisce about our time together and how wonderful being in love with me was. Your heart will never accept that it was not real.

That crack, that fracture, that tiny chunk that remains from your frenetic and devastating time with me shall always remain. It is through it that I can return as I slip, shadow-like into your heart through that unhealed wound. That is why we did what we did; so, we always had a way back in.

You will have to maintain that vigilance for the rest of your life. Our polluting influence, if ever allowed near you again, will creep and trickle through the hole that will never seal. You are consigned to a lifetime of wariness and maintain your defenses because that damage is permanent."

Breaking Free From a Narcissistic Partner: Strategies and Advice

By this point in our journey to better understand narcissistic individuals, one thing should be crystal-clear: there is no chance for a long-term relationship with a person that has NPD. Any "love story" with such individual will end up with heartbreak, shattered dreams, and maybe even years of your life wasted away.

Even when the victim is held tightly in the narcissist's grasps and is forced to accept the reality that he/she wants, deep down, they are aware of the hopeless situation they are in. No matter how hard you might try to deny the truth and rationalize the actions of a narcissist, in the end, it all boils down to the fact that you fell in love with someone that never existed. A charming, wonderful person that promised you the moon and the stars, and you, a kind-hearted individual with a lot of love in your heart to give, trusted him/her. The reality that your soulmate was "fabricated" by a sick, malicious person is absolutely mind-shattering and heartbreaking, for anyone that has to go through it. The trauma eats you up from the inside, even months after the relationship has ended, and the experience changes you in ways you never knew were possible.

No matter how strong-willed, independent, confident someone was before entering into a relationship with a narcissist, the experience steals all of these good things away from you, reducing you to a shadow of your old self, an empty shell that feels hopeless. Not even celebrities are safe from the grasp of abusive relationships. Reese Witherspoon admitted in an interview with Oprah, to have been involved in an emotionally abusive relationship at a young age, also adding that leaving the said relationship was the hardest decision she ever had to make. Stacey Solomon, the presenter of *Loose Women*, has as well been outspoken about her abusive experience, going as far as describing on the program how it changed her, "I was in an abusive relationship, and it makes you forget who you are. It made me feel like I'd never be the same person again. No matter what I do, I'll always be this weird version of myself. A part of me does begrudge that person for taking that away from me. If someone says something over and over again, it can embed in you."

Another famous example, that might come as a surprise, is actor Johnny Depp. He was in a physically and emotionally abusive relationship with actress Amber Hart, but, because our society is biased to believe that only men can be abusers, people believed his now ex-wife's lies, and he was blamed for months of being the perpetrator. Hart used his fame and money to propel herself up, and even proudly advocated as a member of the #MeToo movement. It took several hours of video evidence, multiple witnesses, hospital bills, domestic violence reports, and even Hart herself confessing to attacking her partner in two instances, to make the public accept the fact that Depp was the victim all along.

So, to reiterate my point, abuse can happen to anyone, regardless of gender or popularity. Nothing makes us immune in this world filled with wolves in sheep's clothing. It sounds scary and hard to accept, but this is the reality of it. You are not at fault for putting your trust in a mentally deranged person, because you had no way of knowing their real self at the time. And when you did start noticing the truth, you were already strapped in the horror ride of your life, with little to no way out in sight.

Unfortunately, the only way to put an end to narcissistic abuse is for the victim to initiate the break-up, as soon as he/she realizes that their partner is a narcissist. Break-ups take a lot of time, resilience, strength, effort, will-power, and support. It will take every single bit of energy that you may have left, after the constant abuse in your relationship, and, even when the break-up is done, the effective escape is only halfway done. Keep in mind that victims are emotionally and psychologically addicted to their partners and thus, very vulnerable to hoovering attempts. You may have to go through this 'break-up' 20 odd times until you build up the strength necessary to reject any reconciliation attempts. As time goes by, you will become more and more powerful. However, the only way in which you can break-off the control that the narcissist has over you is by adopting a **No-Contact** stance (or a low/limited contact if that's not possible).

No-Contact is the only solution that prevents relapse into the abusive, intoxicating relationship, and it is the first real step towards getting back control over your life. Think of a relationship with a narcissist as an addiction. You know that it's toxic and harmful. Even if it provides pleasures (in this case small episodes of "love" that makes you feel validated), a long-term relationship could ruin you and destroy you as a person. You realize that it needs to stop, but addiction messes with our brain in such a way that it is very hard to put an end to it. And in order to escape that addiction, you need to stay free of that toxic substance that your brain craves, or in this case, that toxic person. That's why **No-Contact** should be your first step. Your mind and body need to "detox" in order to truly start healing. Every contact you have with the narcissist, post-breakup, is equivalent to you taking in a small quantity of that "drug" back into your system, which is why the danger to "relapse" is so high in these situations. That little dose will have you wanting more, and after a long, emotionally draining fight to leave them, you will have to fight again, and again to make sure that you stay on the right track.

"**No-Contact**" keeps danger at a safe distance as long as you have the power to implement it. However, each situation is different in its own way. If there are children involved, you can't deny them the right to have both parents in their life.

Even though I will go on to present multiple strategies of "escaping" an abusive relationship that might fit most cases, please take the time to find and pick the one that's most suitable for your current situation. Take into consideration how bad your relationship has become, your level of self-respect, and when you consider that enough is enough.

Cold turkey

This term describes the abrupt cease of substance dependence. Which means you are basically stopping all contact with your abusive partner, leaving no room for reconciliation - thus ceasing your addiction of being in a relationship with said person.

Just as it goes for drugs or other addictive substances, abruptly ceasing your intake will lead to secondary effects. You will miss your partner; be tempted to give them another chance; think about the good times and forget the bad ones; or have the tendency to blame yourself for the situation. It's important that you don't give in and keep avoiding any sort of contact with your ex-partner.

This strategy is most suitable for abusive relationships with an element of physical violence / extreme emotional abuse; and in which you don't have other things linking you to the abuser (a family, monetary dependency, co-owned properties).

Gradually stepping away

This strategy is best for situations in which you can't immediately stop all contact with your narcissistic partner (maybe you are living together or there is another situation that prevents you from going "no contact").

Be very careful when you start limiting your contact with the narcissist as he or she will notice and try their best to change your mind. They might go through another round of idealization and love bombing or start playing games with your mind- anything really, just to keep you from leaving and to keep control over you. Remind yourself that nothing that comes out of the mouth of a narcissist is ever true.

Stop rationalizing his/her lies and validating them as truths, they are counting on that.

Stop making excuses for their unnatural behavior and giving them the benefit of the doubt. His/her actions are not your responsibility. You should not have to bear the weight of his/her mistakes.

Be resilient and remember that you are only a minor character in his/her drama show. Your relationship is just a game they play, and nothing more. You don't deserve to be treated like that. No one does.

No going back

In this strategy, the victim does something drastic that for them would make it hard or nearly impossible to go back into the relationship because the consequences of doing that would outweigh the temptation.

This "drastic" action needs to have special meaning for you, and it could be something as simple as changing your Facebook relationship status or as hard as writing a "goodbye" heartfelt message (in which you can pour all of your emotions and cleanse your soul) to your partner, followed by a stern no contact stage. Another thing you can try doing is telling your family or your trusted friend that you have chosen to break things off and explain why (even if you do it in vague terms). The shame you would subject yourself to if you accept him/her back after "exposing" him/her to your close one, could be more than enough to keep your mind far away from fantasies of getting back together.

Breaking point

This is more of a natural response rather than a method per se. It literally means that the victim has reached their breaking point: they realized that they are in a cycle of abuse that keeps on looping and that their partner will never change. They have gone through with it so many times that they are simply too tired to keep ongoing. Your self-respect reanimates from this slumber, and you realize that you deserve better.

When reaching your breaking point, a good idea is to write down your feelings and thoughts, so you will have something to go back to, and re-read whenever you feel tempted to go back into the abusive relationship. Go full "no contact" and be strong. Focus on the future and all the good things that are going to happen from now on in your life. The past should remain a closed door.

Deal-Breaker Evidence

This particular method is an absolute last resort and is not going to apply to everyone. It works best for a relationship that is already pretty much destroyed but to which you are extremely attached and can't seem to let go. You've also done no-contact multiple times and keep relapsing.

The key element for this strategy is to have a strong suspicion that your partner is cheating but you are denying the signs that you see. This ties in with the cognitive dissonance that we mentioned earlier. You can see the peculiar signs but are not fully acknowledging them or don't want to explore further because if you happen to be right, it's going to cause a world of pain.

Before you do explore further, this must be your 'line in the sand moment.' You've most likely had other lines in the sand that have been crossed by your narcissistic partner, and you keep moving the line for them letting them get away with their bad behavior. If this is not the 'line in the sand,' what is? How far are you going to keep moving the line? Deep down, you MUST know within yourself that if your suspicion does turn out to be true, you will feel too hurt and heartbroken to continue clinging to the relationship.

You're most likely never going to get a confession from your abuser. Why would your abuser hand you back your freedom on a silver platter? They're not going to. These people do not feel remorse, guilt or empathy. They want to keep you entangled forever. So if you do decide to go down this road, your abuser's kryptonite is their phone and computer. Social media has made it very convenient for the narcissist to have multiple 'projects' on the go simultaneously.

Does your abuser put their phone face down on the table all the time?

Does your abuser act weird when they get a message from someone?

Does your abuser have the text preview removed?

Does your abuser always have their phone on silent?

Does your abuser let you know their password to their phone and computer?

Does your abuser turn off notifications when they are around you?

Does your partner have communication apps hidden in strange places on their phone?

These are things to take note of. When someone has something to hide, they act strange.

"When you tell the truth, you don't have to remember anything." So, when someone is lying or hiding something from you, they have to spend energy to maintain this lie.

If you do happen to find what your gut may have been telling you, let the emotions out. There is no shame in crying. Allow yourself to grieve and let this be the end. This was the final straw for you, and now you are set free, as you realize that from this point there is no way the relationship can go on.

Co-parenting with a narcissist

When kids are in the picture, it is very important to take into consideration ways in which you can continue to "parent" along with a narcissistic partner in a safe way that does not endanger them or you, for the matter. Going no-contact can be very difficult, especially if your children are still young and incapable of understanding that one of their parents is not behaving properly. Seek the help of a therapist to work up together how you can be a functional family and do what's best for your children.

A helpful suggestion that may work for you is getting a trusted mediator who essentially acts as a middle-man for you, and that way you are able to completely remove yourself from being contacted by your ex-partner.

Detachment

Detachment is the process that any victim of any kind of abuse needs to go through, for their own good. It means understanding and accepting that your partner is not good for you and will never be. In other words, it means *letting go*.

We can boil down detachment to four distinct stages:

1. Stop taking the blame for everything your partner does and realize they are not perfect. In this stage, you also come to the realization that the relationship will never be how you envisioned it, and you stop seeing your partner through rose-tinted glasses. Reality hits you hard.

2. In stage two, you are still emotionally attached to your partner, but you start experimenting a wide array of other feelings: frustration, anger, and resentment. You begin to fight back and stop complying to their every wish. This stage is marked by an abundance of conflicts, as a result to you fighting back, and by doubting everything that your partner says, no longer allowing yourself to be the puppet in his/her one-man show.

3. The third stage is centered around you and your "revival." You are starting to regain some of your confidence and respect, and you begin to actively plan your break up. Now you are able to see your partner for the abuser and monster that he/she truly is.

4. And lastly, the final stage is cutting all ties with the narcissist. You physically move away from your partner, and you keep all communication lines closed. From here on starts the time of healing and slowly rebuilding yourself.

Just because these stages are presented in a logical manner, it doesn't make it any simpler to go from stage 1 to stage 4. It's way too easy to get stuck somewhere between stage 1 and 2, and therefore, allow yourself to enter a loop of endless temporary break-ups. You need a lot of will power and strength if you want to move forward.

I already presented some strategies that might help you break free from the influence of a narcissist, but let's now go through some general ideas and advice, coming from both specialists and from people that had to undergo the same process as you - victims that rose above their traumatic experiences and managed to re-discover themselves.

Your value as a human being can only be determined by you

A lot of victims spend months or even years of their lives trying to reach the high standards of their narcissistic partner, only to be told repeatedly that they are not good enough. People are not perfect, and they never will be. Everybody makes mistakes, but that does not mean that our value as human decreases in any way. Not being perfect does not certify abuse.

A narcissist knows exactly what your insecurities are and how to use them against you. They will try to make you addicted to their validation, giving them the power to put us down or lift us up. But in reality, the only opinion that should matter is your own. You are the only person that is allowed to assess your value as an individual. Trust your gut and your beliefs. Stay true to yourself. Respect yourself and acknowledge your achievements. No one should be allowed to rob you of your identity. If someone doesn't love you for the way you are and forces you to change, then you are better off without them.

You are good enough.

Feed your "escaping" thoughts

When you get to the point in which you realize that the relationship is not going anywhere and your partner is not the person you want to grow old with, you start thinking about breaking up. No matter what, keep thinking about leaving your abusive partner. You reap what you sow, so if you keep feeding your mind these thoughts, you will start gaining more confidence about your decision. And you will feel, deep inside, that it's the right thing to do.

Whenever you are in doubt, close your eyes and remember all the times in which your partner made you feel unhappy. All the excuses you had to make for them, to your friends, family, or other people. Remember all the times they did not take responsibility for their actions and blamed you instead. How much shame can one person take in before it destroys them on the inside?

Don't get charmed away by nice memories of times that are long gone. There is no future for someone living in the past.

Trust yourself

Victims of narcissistic abuse are in an environment in which they have to constantly explain their every word and action, getting to the point where they doubt themselves so much that they feel that their every decision is wrong. This is one of the reasons why it's so hard to leave. Even when they have the decision in their mind, they still counter-attack it with arguments, often fed by the narcissists into their mind, and they can't find a logical reason as to why they should trust themselves.

You don't need to answer to anyone, or to worry about whether or not your decision will turn out to be a good one. Someone times you just know, what's the right thing to do. You feel it in your heart before you pass it through your mental analysis. However, your partner is a cunning manipulator. They will try to chip away at your decision and make you feel doubtful by bombing you with whys and hows. To which it is perfectly acceptable to say, "I don't know." It will spare you the need to explain yourself in the face of a person that would never understand, and it also leaves a door open for future knowledge. A tiny hopeful glimpse of a better future is hidden between that "I don't know."

Get second unbiased opinions

When you are in a relationship with a narcissist you are unknowingly made to live in an almost alternate reality, created by your abusive partner. He or she constantly tells you what you should think or what you should do, leaving you with almost no space to think for yourself. And because he/she already made sure to isolate yourself from your friends and family, making sure you feel guilty whenever you go out with anyone besides him/her, you often have no one else to give you honest/unbiased insight on the relationship. Even when you do step up and see your friends/family, you might still protect your abuser and avoid putting him/her in a bad light, because that's how narcissistic manipulation works.

Asking for opinions from friends that you may have in common with your partner's is pretty much pointless. Most of them live in the same warped reality as you and your partner. In psychological terms, they are called "flying monkeys," a term which describes people that believe in a narcissist's fake persona and that are very open to participating in smear campaigns - something that a narcissist does post-break-up. In other words, you can't trust them. The best place to ask for second opinions is from a couple's therapist or just a regular therapist, that will listen to what you have to say and give you the full dissection of your relationship. Getting feedback from someone that is not in the loop of the narcissist is very valuable, as it will help you see your relationship for what it truly is - an abusive bond.

No one is special

Narcissists have this belief that they are unique creatures that grace the earth with their presence. And they will also make sure to make you believe that what you and him/she have is special and unique and that there is no one else in the whole entire world, better than you two. You need to understand the reason why he/she is feeding you that information: to make you feel isolated. If there is no one like you and him, then you have no one to turn to and ask for advice. No one to help you understand the situation you are in.

It's hard to see things from the outside when your mind is controlled by such a powerful individual. Even if someone else intervenes and tries to show you the true nature of your relationship, you will have a hard time believing it. You need to see it for yourself, with your own two eyes. And the only way to do that is through actively seeking information. Search for your deep dark worries regarding your relationship and you will find articles relating to narcissism. You will start putting two and two together. You will begin to understand what your partner is actually saying and why he/she is doing what they are doing. Understanding helps you break free from the illusion and see reality.

The truth is that no one is special, or more special than other wonderful people that are out there. The sole idea that there are others like you, is very comforting. You are not alone in your struggles.

Accept your feelings

As you break up with your narcissistic partner once and for all, don't expect a wave of instant happiness to come your way. Your bond with your former partner, as flawed as he/she was as a person, was strong. You had moments of happiness and sadness. After all that happened, you might feel hurt, confused, frustrated, and even angry at yourself for allowing this experience to happen.

The only way in which you can heal and move forward is by allowing yourself to go through each and every feeling. It's perfectly acceptable to grieve. Just think for a second about all the things that you have lost: a partner that you love despite everything, a part of you that you will never get back, months or years of emotional investment, maybe your hopes and dreams that your narcissistic partner discouraged you from pursuing.

The pain gets better in time, as you start to forgive yourself and regain your hope for the future. Grieving is the human thing to do, and it is not in any shape or form shameful. Allow yourself the time to handle your emotions in the right way. Re-connect with friends and family, you stopped seeing when you got into your relationship.

Smear campaigns

I've mentioned a little while ago "smear campaigns," so let's see what those are about. In an effort of trying to keep the abuse going, a narcissist will go out into the world and tell every single person you know, from your family to your friends, co-workers, basically anyone they can get in touch with, their version of the break-up. Because during the relationship, the narcissist pressed you to not share many details regarding your interaction with him/her, it is very easy for this malicious person to spread misinformation. They will slander you and blame you for every bad thing that happened in your relationship, smearing your name. This gossiping gets him/her the attention and sympathy she/he deserves (or at least thinks she/he deserves), while also making you out to be the bad guy - a clever way to pressure you back into the relationship and in their grasp.

Expect the smear campaign and don't get intimidated by it. You do not need to waste time trying to convince everyone who did what etc. The truth will reveal itself over time. Your friends and family will always value your word above anyone else's.

The narcissist's next victim

You need to truly understand the fact that narcissists always plan ahead. While being with you, they are already planting the seeds for their next "harvest." Having a supply is necessary for the narcissist's survival. Without people to leech off of they are nothing.

So, they always have multiple potential victims at hand, out of fear that your relationship with him/her will end, or in case they get "bored" with you. They have a backup "harem" - a group of women/men ready to satisfy the narcissist's needs, at their disposal. The advances of today's technology only serve as a helping hand for the predatory narcissist. Thanks to Instagram, Facebook, and other social networks, or dating apps such as Tinder, the narcissist has now the possibility to "sell" their perfect version of themselves. They get followers that admire them unconditionally, and out of these huge masses of adorers, there are bound to be a few that the narcissist can easily manipulate, by simply making them feel special. We see cases like this more and more nowadays. Women/men or even minors being swept from their feet by their idol, just for them to be used and exploited. It's hard to fight back when you have a person that you genuinely admire/look up to, that knows how to easily manipulate you and use that admiration to their benefit.

Besides "helping" narcissists find victims, studies show that the rise of social media might also contribute to the rise of narcissism rates in youths, giving them an audience that boosts their self-esteem over the normal limits and making them develop that false sense of entitlement, often considered as an early sign of NPD. However, these studies are still in a very early stage, and we can't say for certain that social media "popularity" increases the risk of developing narcissism.

The Healing Process

One thing that must be very clear in your mind is that recovery from narcissistic abuse is very tricky. It takes a lot of time and effort, and in truth, the pain that you feel inside never goes away completely. Sure, it gets muted by other feelings, and you become stronger, capable of dealing with it in better, healthier ways. And yet, it remains. A chapter of your life that you can't ignore or forget. Going into recovery and expecting to go back to your old self is wrong. This experience changed your life so much that you are simply unable to re-become that person. The old "you" is gone. And that's fine. You now get the chance to reinvent yourself, a new "you" that has become stronger and wiser, as a result of what has happened to you.

In order to heal from complex trauma, a person must work through the phases of trauma recovery (not to be mistaken with the popular "five stages of grief," which are not extremely accurate despite their usage in pop culture).

Stage 1

Also known as "The emergency stabilization phase," in this first stage, the victim is extremely confused. They made the decision or were forced to go "no contact" with their narcissist, and now they are doubting themselves. The memories of the abuse are still fresh in the victim's mind and are in a continuous state of overstimulation - something that is also happening because the narcissist might still be trying to get in contact with you through mutual friends.

For someone that went through daily, severe emotional abuse, being calm and relaxed is a foreign feeling. Their normality re-defined itself as "being abused" while in the relationship, and once that happens it's hard to realize what normality should really look like. The victim still feels as if she/he needs to answer to their abusive partner for whatever they do/say, and that makes them extremely vulnerable.

In this first stage, what a victim most needs are support and reassurance. They need people actively telling them they made the right decision and helping them build back their self-confidence and trust in their decisions.

Stage 2

This is the start of effective recovery. The victim starts getting their energy back, instead of being continuously sucked out of them - something that a narcissist does. The victim's personality and emotions start showing signs of coming back, albeit timidly.

However, this stage is also dangerous. As the victim starts sorting out their feelings, they start experiencing bouts of anger and frustration, both towards their abuser and themselves, for allowing the abuse to happen. If the victim falls into this trap of self-blaming themselves, she/he might slip right back into stage one, unable to move forward through the stages of trauma recovery. The victim needs proper support, meaning specialized individuals, not social media support groups or friends. Relying too much on such forms of support might eventually become a setback in a victim's recovery process. A therapist knows how to properly guide someone through understanding and accepting their feelings - this is the sort of support that a victim desperately needs!

Stage 3

By this point, the victim is doing great as a matter of recovery. They are on their way towards rebuilding their identity, even if their trauma still makes it hard for them to move on. In this stage, the victim might slip into the dangerous act of giving the narcissist too much credit or trying to come up with an excuse for his/her actions. Thoughts like "we are both to blame for the fact that our relationship did not work out" and "he/she is a victim too, is not his/her fault for being this way" are perfectly reasonable for a person that is overly kind and compassionate, but you must understand that they are not true. It is just the good heart of the victim trying to find reasons to justify the actions of a morally abnormal person.

Still, in stage 3, the victim starts building up their confidence, even though they still feel in a strange way compelled to get back in touch with the narcissist. Not for reconciliation, but for an explanation. They want closure, or deep in their hearts they hope that the narcissist has changed (they never do). Be extremely careful when you get to this point in your recovery. You must keep the "no contact" strategy going (unless you have a family with them or something else that binds you two) or you become vulnerable to falling right back into the cycle of abuse.

Don't forget who you are dealing with: a manipulator, a predator, an opportunist. Not a lover that misses you and wants you back. If you get to this point, I would recommend doing some extensive research on narcissists to better understand how they "function."

Stage 4

At this point, the victim is capable to look back at their abusive experience and analyze it in an objective manner, without getting emotional about it. Feelings of anger and confusion are long gone. All that's left is the bare skeleton of a failed relationship that was not your fault.

When you are in stage 4, you are very aware of your emotions, your internal transformation, and you might even help others that are in earlier stages of their recovery. Although you have managed to build back an identity from the ashes of your old self, there might still be times in which you will slip back into negative feelings regarding yourself and doubt your capabilities of making choices. This doubt and tendency to belittle yourself is just another effect of narcissistic abuse, although you may not recognize it as such. Remind yourself that you are not that person anymore - you have grown, and you have gone so far from the vulnerable individual that was just fresh out of an abusive relationship.

This just comes to show how deep and long-lasting are the effects of narcissistic abuse. Patience and resilience are key.

Stage 5

A victim of abuse that gets to this point is able to see things as they are. They know who they are: their limits and their strengths. They are able to assess their own value as humans and individuals, wiping clean from their minds the lies and depreciations of the narcissist.

When you recover from the abuse, you will have a deep understanding of what it means to be in a healthy relationship and how one is supposed to look like. You know your worth, and you respect yourself enough to not let anyone else walk all over you and undermine you. You know how to stand up for yourself and demand to be treated right. Some degree of caution is still advised since narcissists, and other emotional predators are everywhere. You have already proven to be the sort of empathic, kind-hearted person that this nasty type of person is drawn to, so be very careful. It is true that you have become stronger and more aware of how to recognize this type of people before you get entangled with them. Yet, it's better to be safe than sorry.

Your future is in your hands

While it is good to be aware of these stages of recovery, they are still a theory. They tell you how your recovery is supposed to go, they tell you little to nothing about how you are supposed to get there, except for employing the help of a specialized professional to sort through your emotional issues.

During the relationship, the narcissist became the focus point of your life. You had spent all of your time either with them or communicating with them through cute texts and never-ending phone calls. You went on amazing dates that you will probably never forget for the rest of your life. All this happens in the idealization phase, but that stage alone does enough as a matter of isolating you from friends and family and keeping you away from chasing your dreams. Anything else, but the narcissist, became secondary in your life. Your work might have suffered along with your relationships.

But now, your focus should be coming back to your own person. Remember your goals and ambitions! Remember your habits and the things you used to do for fun! Go back to those and re-activate the dopamine - the hormone of happiness, in your mind. You don't need to rely on the narcissist anymore to offer you validation and pleasure. Engage in your favorite activities and take back your happiness in your own hands - something that will make it easier to maintain the no contact rule with your abusive partner.

Here are a few ways in which you can naturally increase your dopamine levels:

- Adopt a diet rich in proteins (turkey, beef, eggs, legumes, dairy) and low in saturated fats (such as butter, animal fat, coconut oil). Proteins are essential because amino acids found in them help with the production of dopamine, while saturated fats can negatively impact the dopamine system.
- Have an exercise routine as it improves mood.
- Make sure that you get a healthy amount of sleep so that your dopamine receptors don't lose their ability to work properly. A good sleep schedule ensures that your dopamine levels stay balanced.
- Take in some sunlight to boost both your dopamine levels and subsequently your mood. Be careful to not go overboard with it as excessive sun exposure could cause skin damage.
- Listen to music - it actually increases levels in the reward and pleasure areas of your brain.
- Have a discussion with a specialist and determine (through some blood work) whether or not your body is in need of vitamin supplements. For example, deficient levels of vitamin B or iron could negatively affect your dopamine production. If you want to go all-natural, you can get Vitamin B from meat, dairy products, peas, leafy green vegetables, and eggs, while iron can be found in fish, turkey, broccoli, and spinach. Consult a nutritionist for more

options if necessary.

Besides making sure that your dopamine levels are kept at optimum levels, there are other things that you should look out for when healing a traumatized brain. Firstly, you should know that a brain that has gone through trauma works differently than a healthy one. To put it in simple terms, a traumatized brain has its "thinking center" under-activated because the narcissist fed you what to think at all times; the "emotional regulation center" is also under-activated as it had to be, in order for you to sustain the huge amount of constant trauma; and the "fear center" is overly activated - for obvious reasons. A brain that is in this condition has difficulties with assessing information and with managing emotions, even if the person actively tries to calm down and take it easy when they feel overwhelmed. Getting your brain back to its original state is hard, and it takes a lot of time and repetition. You will require the help of a psychotherapist that specializes in trauma, and who knows how to use evidence-based methods that can produce positive changes in your brain.

Secondly, you will have to make some changes in your regular, day to day life. Learn/practice relaxation techniques, such as meditation, that deactivate the fear center of your brain. It will not only help you relax, but it also gives you the chance to focus on yourself and restore your self-image. It will aid you in forgiving yourself and accepting yourself, which is crucial for recovery. You can also try to practice breathing techniques, other types of self-discovery methods, maybe yoga - it would also offer a chance for meeting new people and getting in tune with your spiritual side.

And last, but not least, in order to help not only your brain but yourself to advance further on this recovery journey, there are some additional changes/things you should try or at least consider doing. It's nothing scary, don't worry. Some of these things will bring you a lot of joy, even if others might be a bit hard to do at first. Smother yourself with self-love, self-respect, and self-care in order to start feeling good about yourself again. You have been through a lot. The narcissist has scooped out an enormous amount of self-worth from you in an attempt to make you a serving slave to them. We need to refill your self-worth and get you feeling good about yourself again and there are many ways we can do that:

- Sit down and create a list of achievable goals, something you can work toward and look forward to. Think of all the things that you wanted to accomplish prior to the relationship or all the interests and passions that you have ignored while you were under the narcissist's influence. There should be at least a few things that pop in your mind. Just be careful to focus on achievable things - be mindful of what you can do and don't try to force your limits. Goals give you a purpose in life, and right now you desperately need one, to motivate you and keep you on track.

- Be physically active even if you are not the type of person that particularly enjoys sports. Besides improving your dopamine levels, physical activity also prompts your brain to secrete endorphins, substances that combat the cortisol that was overly produced due to stress. Choose a type of activity that you would truly enjoy, such as dancing - which has a lot of great benefits to it. However, try to consider first a sport/activity that can be done in teams or with a group of people, as it would be very beneficial for you to socialize. Especially with yoga, where most people are very positive and mindful of other people's feelings. It will help you fend off all that negativity that you have gathered from the traumatic experience.

- Get back in contact with the people in your life. This might be very hard at first because you will have to explain your situation and therefore, "expose" the true nature of your relationship. For you, this will be a bitter-sweet victory as it offers up a cocktail of emotions: shame, anger, relief, and gratitude. But you will be surprised to see that most of the people in your life were already aware of your hurting, but they either decided to not interfere or if they tried, you may have pushed them away. Trust your friends and family. They know you and the type of person you are. They will be there for you to support and love you in your time of need.

- To further expand on this point, be selective with the energy you surround yourself with. Yes, the narcissist may have shattered your boundaries in the past but it is time to rebuild these boundaries from the ground up. It is time to no longer tolerate an ounce of negativity or put-downs from anyone. By surrounding yourself with good energy and vibes only, you put yourself on to the fast track for a healthy recovery.

- Re-engage with your old hobbies that you had prior to the relationship, especially if they are creative or related to the outdoors. Writing, painting, and sculpting might offer you a way to express yourself, helping you re-define your lost identity and maybe get rid of some of that emotional baggage. Video games and reading gives you an entrance into a different world, one in which you can relax and have a good time. Physical activity keeps your body occupied while your mind roams free. Going on walks, hikes or treks gives you the opportunity to be in nature, which is known to be therapeutic for both our minds and our souls. If you don't want to re-engage with an older hobby then start a brand new one from scratch, be it creative or active. Even starting a new business could give you a great opportunity to focus your mind on something both positive and stimulating. Who knows? Maybe you'll even get a new career out of it.

- Escape for a bit from your everyday life. You've been through a lot. It's perfectly fine if you need to go away for some time, in a new exciting place to heal and recharge your depleted batteries. It could be a very refreshing experience to get in contact with a different culture, meet new people, and just explore the wonders that our beautiful world has to offer. Your mind will thrive in a new, exciting environment!

- Laugh as much as you can. Laughter is the ultimate medicine for both your mind and soul. It makes your brain secrete substances that make you feel good and it puts you into a good mood. Go out with your fun-loving friends, see your favorite comedy movies/TV serials, watch stand-up comedy shows, or do anything else that will put a smile on your face.

- Start reading empowering materials. Read self-development books that present motivational stories and good advice. If you feed your mind with positive, empowering materials, which is good-quality food for your brain, you are being proactive in helping your mind heal.

- And last but not least, go splurge on yourself. Get that massage you've always been meaning to get but never made the time for. Get that manicure. Buy that outfit you've always wanted to buy. Try that new hairstyle you've been thinking about getting. Let this be your own stamp of authority that you will not allow yourself to ever be walked over again and your self-worth is not something to be toyed with.

To end this chapter on a good note, here are some "healing

affirmations" that you can use as tools to help you move away from the negative mindset that the abuse caused. Use them at the beginning of every morning to boost your mood, hope, belief, trust, and your self-esteem. By using positive daily affirmations, you are re-wiring your subconscious mind which in turn will result in a more desirable and positive reality.

"I am healing one step at a time."

"I am a good person, that deserves love, affection, and respect."

"I surround myself with positive energy only."

"I am worthy of the beautiful things the Universe has to offer me."

"I am open to the beautiful things the Universe has to offer me."

"I love myself."

"I surround myself with people who respect me and my boundaries."

"I am grateful for my friends and family."

"I am putting the past behind me, and I will focus on the present and future."

"I am making a priority out of my recovery."

"I can trust my mind and my instincts to lead me towards making the right decision."

"My boundaries are strong, and nothing can make me overstep them."

"My friends and family will always love and support me, no matter what."

"I choose to become a better version of myself each and every day."

"I continue to learn and educate myself."

"I am improving each and every day."

Conclusion

Here we are, at the end of it all. You now know what a narcissist is and how they "work."

They are unable of feeling "love" towards anyone else but themselves. They live for the sole purpose of having their needs and expectations met, and they are under the false belief that the world owes them something. A relationship with a narcissist is just a fancy way of spelling "emotional and psychological abuse" and nothing more. All the love, support, care, and empathy are one-sided, from you towards them. They leech off of you and feed on your adoration and insecurities. You are their tool and nothing more.

However, no matter how hard it may be, you can always escape. Despite what your abuser is trying to make you believe, you are still in control of your own life and choices. You can choose to leave. Why? Because you had enough. Because you are a human being and you deserve to be loved, respected, and taken care of. You deserve to get in return as much as you give. Have the courage to break off the chain! Your friends and family will be there to support you. Your mind and your heart will heal. You will be fine! But your life won't really "start" until you choose to go.

I have given you ways in which you can safely leave an abusive relationship. Whatever you may choose, remember that NO CONTACT is the best way to go if you have no deeper ties linking you to your abuser. No contact means no temptation. It means that you are protecting yourself from the possibility of ever going back to the cycle of abuse. The narcissist won't make it easy on you, by hoovering and trying to reach you in subtle ways, but don't give in. Every time he/she tries to come back, remember the way he/she made you feel - not at the start of the relationship but at the end of it. Remember the sadness, the pain. The shame of having to come up with explanations on his/her behalf. The frustration of taking responsibility for something they have done. And think about the future you want: your goals, your plans, all the things you want to try. All the people that will be there for you. Think about a future in which you can love and be loved back by someone that genuinely cares about you!

You deserve to be happy. You deserve to be loved. You are capable of making the best choices for yourself and you must trust your decisions. Recovery is hard but it will happen - with slow but confident little baby steps. You will never go back to being who you were *before*, but you have the power to decide who you are going to be. Have faith in your own abilities. Don't be afraid to ask for the help of others, both professionals and regular people. Support groups and friends will always be there when you need them.

You are a strong, wonderful, kind-hearted person. And you will be fine. Allow yourself the time you need to heal and take care of yourself!

I wish you the best of luck with your journey and recovery, and if you found this information in any way helpful to you and your situation, please let me know in the form of a review. It gives me great satisfaction to know that I have been able to help someone along their troublesome journey as I know how hard it can be to free yourself from the web of a narcissist. This will also help other victims out there desperate for a helping hand.

Thank you

Lightning Source UK Ltd.
Milton Keynes UK
UKHW021847271022
411196UK00011B/1460